The Weight Of the Wait

God's Unexpected Purpose
for Life's Hardest Seasons

SAM WEGNER

LUCIDBOOKS

The Weight of the Wait: God's Unexpected Purpose for Life's Hardest Seasons

Copyright © 2025 by Sam Wegner

Published by Lucid Books in Houston, TX

www.LucidBooks.com

All rights reserved. No part of this publication may be reproduced, stored in a retrieval system, or transmitted in any form by any means, electronic, mechanical, photocopy, recording, or otherwise, without the prior permission of the publisher, except as provided for by USA copyright law.

Unless otherwise indicated, scripture quotations are taken from the (NASB®) New American Standard Bible®, Copyright © 1960, 1971, 1977, 1995, 2020 by The Lockman Foundation. Used by permission. All rights reserved. www.lockman.org

Scripture quotations marked (ESV) are taken from the ESV® Bible (The Holy Bible, English Standard Version®), copyright © 2001 by Crossway, a publishing ministry of Good News Publishers. Used by permission. All rights reserved.

Scripture quotations marked (KJV) are taken from the King James Version (KJV): King James Version, public domain.

Scripture quotations marked (NIV) are taken from the Holy Bible, New International Version®, NIV®. Copyright ©1973, 1978, 1984, 2011 by Biblica, Inc.™ Used by permission of Zondervan. All rights reserved worldwide. www.zondervan.com The "NIV" and "New International Version" are trademarks registered in the United States Patent and Trademark Office by Biblica, Inc.™

ISBN: 978-1-63296-793-0
eISBN: 978-1-63296-794-7

Special Sales: Most Lucid Books titles are available in special quantity discounts. Custom imprinting or excerpting can also be done to fit special needs. Contact Lucid Books at Info@LucidBooks.com

For Crystal
I would rather wait with no one but you

Contents

Acknowledgments vii

Prologue
The Weight of the Wait 1

Chapter One
Understanding Hope 9

Chapter Two
Redefining Good 31

Chapter Three
Understanding Waiting 51

Chapter Four
Why God Makes Us Wait 77

Chapter Five
Hope-driven Waiting 101

Chapter Six
Waiting Well 131

Chapter Seven
   How to Wait Better 159
Epilogue
   The Wait Continues 183

Endnotes 187

Acknowledgments

Without my lovely wife, Crystal, this book would not exist. She is truly the heroine of this story. All I've ever had to do is wait, but she has carried the burden of waiting in addition to facing pain, disease, and death, which she has done with inimitable grace, hope, and perseverance. If it were not for her dogged determination to continue to serve Jesus and others with all her heart, soul, mind, and strength (regardless of how much or little of the latter she has), I would have never learned these truths about waiting, much less written about them. Thank you, my love, for your enduring faithfulness to our Father and me.

I could have wished for no better brothers in adversity than John Romain, Rick Wilcox, Kyle Souza, and Chris Jurek. They have faithfully waited with me, prayed for me, challenged me, and allowed me to be transparent about my struggles along the journey. When someone like me is sharing, that means having to endure and process some off-the-wall ideas and a LOT of words—hundreds of thousands of them—yet they've done it without reservation or complaint. It was at their encouragement that I undertook the task of writing this book, and their feedback about the content was invaluable. If you are helped by what you find in these pages, you have them to thank; just know that you'll have to get in line behind me and wait a long time for your turn.

I am also indebted to the members of my small group: John, Kathy, Pheba, Ann, Greg, Cherie, David, Caterina, Darin, Jill, Shelly, Monica, and Nathan. They, too, have waited, both for me to finish my long-winded stories which consumed more than my fair share of group time, as well as with me in eager anticipation of what the Lord would do next. I am thankful for their encouragement and the color they have added to my seasons of waiting individually and collectively.

Words are not enough to thank my good friends, pastors Scot Pollok and Shawn Thornton. By simply being faithful to preach the Word of God to the congregations God called them to serve, they unknowingly also ministered to me during some of the darkest and most difficult days of my waiting in the wilderness. They were my lifeline, not unlike the birds that fed Elijah, used by the Lord to deliver specific instruction and encouragement to me exactly when I needed it, not just once, but consistently and repeatedly. Because of them, I learned to look forward with eagerness to my hour-long morning commute and considered it a special treat when traffic was so bad I could finish two sermons in one trip.

Special thanks are due to Sarah Inabnit, my little sister in every way except by birth, who edited the first draft of this manuscript with the candidness that only a sister can express and lovingly made it better.

Thank you to Kenzie Lugenbeel for patiently lending her graphic talents to beautify my rough sketches of the diagrams. Creating a visual representation of someone else's ideas is much more challenging than it seems, especially when that person changes his mind multiple times during the process.

Last, I would like to thank Greg Cryer for asking the question that opened my eyes to a problem I didn't know I had. More than leading to a book, it led to a critical and necessary change in my heart, for which I am eternally grateful.

Prologue

The Weight of the Wait

The room was alive with the buzz of conversation. About thirty of us had gathered at our small group leader's home to visit with some special guests. A missionary family, who had been part of our group for several years before going overseas, was back in town for a brief visit, and everyone was excited to see them again. The gathering was much larger than usual that day because others from the church who wanted to see our missionary friends were also invited. Despite our hosts having a sizable space for us to meet in, it was somewhat challenging to hear at times over the welcome noise of people laughing and conversing.

The missionaries were not the only celebrities present that day; my wife, Crystal, a stage 4 metastatic breast cancer patient, was also in attendance. Although we were about a year removed from any COVID-19 socialization restrictions, we still had to be very careful about limiting her forays into public. However, this occasion warranted an exception, as she shared a special bond with the son of the missionary family, who had been a student of hers in the church's Special Needs ministry. They were both excited to have this opportunity to reconnect. Most of the rest of the attendees, however, weren't aware that Crystal would be there, so her mere presence raised the energy level in the room, turning it into quite the party.

While I enjoy them, gatherings of that nature tend to wear me out quickly, so at a certain point I stepped away from the bulk of the crowd to the kitchen counter to recover and get some refreshments. I wasn't particularly hungry, but eating is a socially acceptable substitute for talking if you need a moment to yourself when you're at a party. Unfortunately, the plate in my hand did not camouflage me as much as I had hoped. A friend of mine, Greg, approached me and initiated a conversation.

Greg was an elder at our church. I had known him for years, as we had daughters about the same age who were friends and grew up together, but we hadn't had more than a passing conversation in a long time. Like everyone else, he was excited to see Crystal come that day and came to me for first-hand information about how we were doing and how he could pray for us.

Crystal's cancer is a chronic condition. At the time of the party, she had been battling it for over seven and a half years, so I had developed a set of semi-prepared responses to questions about her health. It might seem a bit calloused and mechanical to have a battery of pat answers for what are usually genuine caring inquiries, but at times the sheer volume can be overwhelming. It can be very awkward to unload graphic detail on someone only interested in exchanging polite platitudes, so I learned to quickly assess which degree of response was appropriate in a given moment. They varied from superficial generalizations designed to discourage further conversation to in-depth expositions replete with more-than-you-probably-care-to-know-but-you-asked details. Which one I used depended on the context, how much I felt like sharing at the moment, who was asking, and how much I sensed they wanted to know. Judge me if and however you will—I openly admit it was a coping mechanism—but it worked for me.

When Greg asked me how we were coping, I sensed that he genuinely wanted a deeper answer. So, I chose one of my more candid entry points and responded at that level, describing some of our most recent medical challenges in detail. He listened patiently and intently, but I could tell from his face that I hadn't answered the question he was asking. He paused briefly, looked at me intently, and rephrased it: "How are you doing with the weight?"

I pretended that in the din of the other conversations in the room I hadn't understood him clearly, but in reality, the question caught me completely off-guard. To regain my footing, I asked him to repeat it. "How are you dealing with the weight?" he asked.

It's not uncommon for people to ask about me when they ask about her, but it had never been put to me quite that way before. My battery of canned responses was designed to allow me to control the direction of these conversations, yet I suddenly found myself on my heels, reeling in search of a reply. Greg recognized that I was struggling with a burden that I thought I had disguised pretty well and had gently, but quite directly, called me on it. Up to that point, while I felt the heaviness, I never really expressed it, even to myself. I hesitated as my consciousness absorbed the shock of the instinctive response about to leave my mouth. "The heaviest weight is the wait," I said. He nodded understandingly. He knew what I meant.

That was the first time I acknowledged that I had a problem with the idea that my wife would likely die from her disease. We talked openly about the possibility of it from the initial diagnosis. We took care of all the necessary arrangements: wills, powers of attorney, advanced directives. When we received the metastatic diagnosis, the possible became probable, but even that wasn't completely unexpected. My answer to Greg's question revealed that my issue wasn't with how this story would end—it was with how long it was taking to get there.

I know—that sounds awful. That's because it is. It's not much different than Ebenezer Scrooge in Charles Dickens' *A Christmas Carol* who declared that those who would rather die than go to a debtor's prison had better do it and decrease the surplus population. In my defense, meager as it is, I never consciously thought about it that way or had expressed it out loud until Greg unintentionally pulled it out of me.

Instead, I expressed my disdain for waiting in other, seemingly less calloused ways. For example, I frequently wondered out loud if it were better to have advanced warning that you were going to die or for it just to happen suddenly. It's a rather pointless question because the truth is we all know that we're going to die eventually and having more specific information about when it's going to happen doesn't necessarily improve one's attitude and outlook as much as you might think. For instance, in my case, waxing philosophical was my way of trying to hide my weariness behind a conundrum so that it didn't sound like murmuring. In retrospect, I doubt that it fooled anyone much, except me.

The boldest I ever got in expressing my impatience out loud was to complain about pre-grieving, also known as anticipatory grief. It usually manifests after receiving news that death is imminent or inevitable. It causes you to grieve as if the event had already happened when it has not. My attitude when I pre-grieved was that I wouldn't mind it so much if I could bank it and apply it to the actual event later, even though I knew it doesn't work like that. Of course, I would have never said, "Hurry up and decrease the surplus population, hon—I'm getting tired of waiting." That would have definitely made me a horrible person. Thinking it would have been just as bad. Instead, I just felt it. I figured my only option was to suck it up and carry the weight.

You see, waiting has heft to it. It has mass. Just observe people who are waiting, and you'll see it. All you have to do is go to a TSA security line at any airport, a driver's license facility in a major city, or pretty much any attraction at Disney World, and you'll immediately see the burden that waiting puts on people. They can't stand still. They lean on things. They sit down. They eye with jealousy those who paid more to wait less, now regretting a decision that seemed sensible a few hours ago. They start doing other things to distract themselves from the task of waiting. The longer they wait, the more they feel it; when it is finally over, they are exhausted. Even those who seem to have the proverbial patience of Job are not immune to the effects of waiting. You've felt them, just as I have. The weight of the wait is real.

I never really understood that my problem was with waiting and how big it was until Greg coaxed it out of me. However, after I heard those words come out of my mouth, the idea of waiting was constantly in my face. It seemed that every time I opened my Bible, passages about waiting would jump off the page, flashing like they were on an LED billboard. They were everywhere. I wasn't intentionally seeking them out, but God flooded my life with them. Initially, you could have attributed this phenomenon to my hypersensitivity to the topic, but it wasn't just me. It got to a point where I couldn't attend a church service or listen to a podcast without someone referencing waiting. I originally thought the burden I felt was from grief, and to some extent it was, but the more the Lord inundated me with these references, the more I realized that the weight I felt did not come from grieving but instead came from waiting.

Figuring that out didn't help a whole lot. For starters, I don't like waiting. Frankly, I don't know that I've ever met anyone who does. Unfortunately, other than reassuring me I was in good company, that didn't do much to relieve the burden I was bearing. On top of that, waiting is impossible to avoid. There are ways to deal with grief, to process and heal from the pain, to get to a point where it doesn't dominate your every waking moment. Waiting, on the other hand, is inescapable. It's everywhere, touching every facet of your life. It's not something you can get over, because most of the time you don't have any control over it. Before you can stop waiting for one thing, you can easily find yourself in a dozen other queues. Understanding that my issue was with waiting and not grief seemed to serve no purpose other than to constantly rub my nose in my inability to deal with it. Only now, in addition to bearing the burden of waiting, I also began to feel the weight of not knowing what to do about it.

Eventually, I saw a pattern emerging in the constant barrage of Bible verses about waiting. "Those who hopefully wait for Me will not be put to shame" (Isaiah 49:23). "And now, Lord, for what do I wait? My hope is in You" (Psalm 39:7). "My soul, wait in silence for God only, for my hope is from Him" (Psalm 62:5). Time and time again, I saw hope and waiting in the same context, frequently in the same verse.

The notion of hope being directly tied to waiting was something I never considered before, and it intrigued me. As much as I disliked waiting, I liked hope. I intuitively understood that hope should be some antidote to the weight of the wait, which was a very appealing proposition. This, however, presented me with another problem. I thought I had a pretty good grasp on hope and considered myself a hopeful person, yet somehow, I was still being crushed by the weight of my waiting. Something was wrong: my hope wasn't working the way biblical authors like David and Isaiah said it should.

This warranted some additional investigation. If I was ever going to figure out how to deal with the weight of the wait, I needed first to reevaluate my definition of hope.

Chapter One

Understanding Hope

What is hope?

Hope. Simply reading the word "hope" uplifts my spirit; but especially when I'm feeling despondent, frequently all it does is elicit a brief sigh as if to say, "Yeah, it would sure be nice to have some of that right now." At other times, it resonates with and amplifies my dreams, causing me to look to the future with anticipation. I'm certain you can relate to my experience.

You and I aren't the only ones to have pondered the nature of hope. Alexander Pope, an 18th-century English poet, famously wrote, "Hope springs eternal in the human breast."[1] Fyodor Dostoevsky, Russian author of *Crime and Punishment* fame, said, "To live without hope is to cease to live."[2] Whether you feel you have all the hope in the world or that all of it is lost, hope is an essential component of the human psyche. It helps us endure bad times and adds joy in good times. It inspires us to move forward, set challenging goals, and overcome difficult obstacles.

However, not everyone views hope in a positive light. German philosopher Friedrich Nietzsche declared that "hope in reality is the worst of all evils because it prolongs the torments of man."[3] Margaret Weiss, American science fiction and fantasy writer, believes that "hope is the denial of reality."[4] Ironically, even in their skepticism, their words recognize hope's power in our lives, even though they consider it misguided and misplaced.

The problem with hope is that future events do not always materialize in the manner or at the time that we would like them to, leading to disappointment and the belief that hope itself is to blame for our misfortune. Such was the perspective of English politician George Savile, who believed "hope is generally a wrong guide, though it is good company along the way,"[5] and of philosopher Francis Bacon, who declared that "hope is a good breakfast, but it is a bad supper."[6] Intuitively, we understand that suffering a few bad outcomes is not a good reason for abandoning the practice of hoping altogether. Still, the harsh reality that many things in life don't go our way can cause even the most optimistic among us to sometimes equate hope with nothing more than wishful thinking.

This broad spectrum of opinions about hope illustrates that the concept of hope seems to suffer from a phenomenon I call the ambiguity of ubiquitousness—a paradox in which something is so universal and intuitively familiar that it eludes clear definition. In other words, because everyone in the world has ideas, feelings, and experiences we associate with hope, we all believe we know what it is; however, when pressed to articulate those thoughts in a concise and coherent manner, not to mention to apply that definition consistently in real-world situations, we quickly realize that there is widespread confusion about the true nature of hope and the role it should and does play in our emotional, mental, physical, and spiritual well-being.

Therefore, when I began trying to identify where my idea of hope had gone wrong, I started by consulting several online dictionaries, which unfortunately did not provide the clarity I expected. Merriam-Webster defines hope as "to cherish a desire with anticipation, to want something to happen or to be true."[7] The Cambridge Dictionary expands on that idea somewhat: "to want something to happen or to be true and usually have a good reason to think that it might."[8] The Collins Dictionary defines hope as "a feeling of desire and expectation that things will go well in the future,"[9] while the Oxford Advanced American Dictionary describes it as "a belief that something you want will happen."[10] While these definitions sound similar, they are not equivalent.

To quote that great philosopher, Pinocchio

In the sample of definitions listed above, hope is characterized as a desire, the result of a rational thought process, a feeling, and a belief. As I considered how these definitions of hope differ and how they affect our perspective on life, I was drawn to the musings of some of the world's most popular philosophers: songwriters. Though we seldom recognize it as a philosophical expression, music allows us to express feelings and ideas in a way that candidly exposes what we believe about a wide variety of topics. Interestingly, one of the most common of these across all musical styles is hope. Whether we have it and are excited about it, want it but can't find it, or had it and lost it, we can find some crooner in every music genre imaginable whose songs echo how we feel about hope. However, because we tend to relate to music emotionally, we frequently don't realize how much the lyrics of those songs shape how we define hope and what we think about it.

For example, the idea that hope is simply about desires, about wanting good things to happen, immediately causes "When You Wish Upon a Star" from Disney's animated classic, *Pinocchio,* to come to mind. It promises that, if we wish for something hard and sincerely enough, it will come true.[11] Be honest—you've sung that song before; and, at least for a brief moment, at some point in your life, you believed it. Perhaps you still do. It should really come as no surprise that this resonates with us. Even though we acknowledge we do not live in a world where marionettes come to life, we all long for the fairy tale ending. As a result, ironically, sometimes being confronted with the reality that not every story has the outcome we want causes us to double down on our wishes. Driven by our desire to live happily ever after, hope means continuing to wish all our dreams will come true in spite of evidence to the contrary.

On the other hand, if you prefer a more pragmatic approach based on having a good reason to expect good things are going to happen, then perhaps hope is simply realizing you just need to make it to the next day to see things work out. This is more than Pinocchio's wishing on a star—this has a flavor of empirical logic to it. Since you have a reasonable expectation that the sun will come out tomorrow (because it always has), hope means toughing out the bad times because everything will be better in the light of day.

The imagery of the sun rising after a dark night or a gloomy winter serves as a common metaphor for hope. The essence of this way of thinking is that scary, disappointing, or hurtful things, represented by darkness or night, are temporary and will disappear when the sun drives them away. This perspective appears in several well-known songs, such as George Harrison's "Here Comes the Sun" from The Beatles' *Abbey Road* album. If you've ever endured a cold, dreary, depressing winter like those in northern Europe, you can relate to

Harrison's anticipation of a cheery, sunshiny day that warms your face and heart, and restores your belief that everything is going to be all right.[12]

Or, if hope is a feeling, then all we need is some energy, some positive thinking, and maybe a good disco dance rhythm to spur us on to success, as in the title song from the movie *Flashdance*[13], by Irene Cara. The core message of the song and the movie is that we should feel empowered to determine our destiny and bring it to fruition. In fact, in an interview conducted by the BBC in 2013 with Cara about the origins of the song, the artist confirmed that she and co-author Keith Forsey intentionally "used dance as a metaphor for, you know, attaining anything in your life that you want to accomplish."[14]

Is it any wonder that this song spent six weeks at number one on the pop music charts in 1983? I have to admit that I, too, am one of the millions who have belted out its lyrics into a hairbrush mic. After all, who doesn't want to believe that they can make their passions come to life? Isn't that what passion is all about? It feels good to get your heart rate up, get that blood pumping, and be energized with feeling that you can conquer any challenge that comes your way. What's not hopeful about that?

However, if hope is persistently believing something good will happen, then Whitney Houston might have been on to something. In one of her lesser-known songs, *Never Give Up*[15], which was released posthumously on a compilation album in 2012, she talks about a single mother who must work multiple jobs to provide for her daughter. Despite her challenging circumstances and naysayers who tell her she will never succeed or amount to anything meaningful, Houston encourages this mom, and everyone else to whom life has dealt a bad hand, to never give up. The promise here is that things will get better, and miracles will happen, as long as you don't quit.

We all know people like the woman in this song. We respect them. We admire them. We root for them. You might be one of them. They inspire us with their never-say-die, pick-yourself-up, dust-yourself-off, start-all-over-again attitude in the face of overwhelming odds that defies the very presence of the word "quit" in the dictionary. They seem to epitomize hope, overcoming the challenges in their lives with sheer willpower.

Each of these examples puts a different spin on what hope is. They illustrate that how we define hope dictates our perspective on the things that we do and the things that happen to us. Additionally, because we find it so easy to relate to all of them, they demonstrate how susceptible we all are to changing our perspective based on the mood or situation we're in at any given point in time. As I realized how much confusion there is about hope, I began to understand better why it seems to fail us in the most challenging moments of our lives.

The scholarly approach

Personally, I prefer to base my concept of hope on something more scholarly than the wailing of a lovelorn country music singer (regardless of how relatable they may be), so I looked to the American Psychological Association (APA) for a more clinical definition. In the *APA's Dictionary of Psychology*, hope is defined as "the expectation that one will have positive experiences or that a potentially threatening or negative situation will not materialize or will ultimately result in a favorable state of affairs."[16] The APA further explains that, in psychological literature, hope can be viewed as a character strength, an emotion, a component of goal-oriented motivation, a coping mechanism, or a blend of any or all of these elements.

That sounds impressive, but upon reflection I quickly realized it's not as helpful as I was hoping it would be. First, it defers to the context in which hope is expressed or discussed to determine its nature and meaning, a fancy way of saying, "it all depends." Second, the APA definition opens several other cans of worms, specifically, values, ethics, and morals. That's not problematic in itself, because one's understanding of good and bad does indeed impact one's view of hope. The issue lies in its assumption of a shared consensus on what good and bad are without offering a solid foundation for that understanding. As a matter of fact, while the APA's dictionary does contain entries for the words "value," "moral," "ethics," and even "faith," it does not define either "good" or "bad." Suddenly, basing my ideas about hope on Katy Perry's song *Firework* or Kelly Clarkson's *Stronger* doesn't sound so bad, as long as I don't tell anyone where they came from.

Given the inherent ambiguity in the clinical definition, it should be no surprise that the scientific community has just as much difficulty understanding hope as the rest of us. In fact, one researcher in 2003 identified at least 26 different theoretical models for hope in psychological literature.[17] For better or worse, one of those models has emerged over the last three decades as the predominant psychological view of hope. Dr. Charles Richard "Rick" Snyder, a psychologist in the field of positive thinking, is recognized as the father of "hope theory." He authored 15 books on various psychological topics, half of which focused on positive psychology and hope. Snyder viewed hope as a dynamic state of being derived from one's perceived ability to envision pathways to achieve goals and motivate oneself to pursue them. In other words, Snyder believed that hopeful people are highly motivated to identify and implement multiple paths to overcome obstacles that hinder their ability to achieve their objectives[18].

Dr. Snyder developed a twelve-statement, self-analysis tool designed to measure how hopeful a person is and plot that person's relative position on his Hope Scale. The tool asks the subject to rate how true each statement is of them on a scale of 1 to 8. Adding the response values together yields a person's overall hope score. Given the subjective nature of the assessment, rather than reference absolute values, Snyder preferred to speak in broad terms of "high hope" versus "low hope" individuals. Originally conceived as a static trait, Snyder subsequently came to see hope as a dynamic state of being, one that could come and go and vary in intensity depending on various contextual factors. However, he never altered his Hope Scale or the assessment tool to account for those variables.

Although it may seem simple at first, numerous studies have shown Snyder's model is highly effective at predicting academic achievement, emotional well-being, coping mechanisms in response to trauma, and the ability to improve one's socioeconomic status. For example, in 2000, Dr. Snyder conducted a well-known experiment live on the set of *Good Morning America*, where three cast members were challenged to keep their hands submerged in freezing water for as long as possible. After all three eventually gave up, Snyder explained to the national television audience that there is a correlation between hope and pain tolerance, and he revealed that the hope scale assessment, which the cast had taken before the show, accurately predicted how long each of them could withstand the cold water.[19]

Even though Snyder's model seems to hold up remarkably well under scientific scrutiny, it still has flaws. The first and most obvious is that it assumes all humans are goal-oriented and does not account for any other kind of motivation, a limitation that other researchers and Snyder himself eventually recognized. Additionally, the hope scale arguably measures commitment to goal-oriented self-actualization more than it does hope itself. It also fails to reflect the influence that external agents may have on a person's sense of hope, regardless of whether those agents support or oppose the individual's efforts to achieve their goals. The biggest hurdle for me is the fact that the hope scale requires a person to evaluate statements on a sliding scale of truth, which suggests to me that Snyder had a bias towards moral relativism. While that doesn't completely invalidate his research and observations, it does make it difficult for his conclusions to be consistent with a biblical worldview, which is based on the principle of absolute truth.

It's OK—until it's not

Do you see what I mean about hope suffering from the ambiguity of ubiquitousness? All these ideas sound similar at first, but when pressed into practical application they are very different, and the ways they differ are significant. To complicate matters further, my search for definitions was far from exhaustive. There's no telling how many others we could uncover with a little extra effort, but to what end? Certainly, more confusion would do little to provide greater clarity.

At this point, you may have lost all hope of confidently understanding what hope is. With so many people who are better known, more talented, more intelligent, and more accomplished than we are having such difficulty coming to a consensus, what chance do the rest of us stand of making sense of it?

After all, most of us are not quotable authors, famous songwriters, shrewd philosophers, or credentialed psychologists. Most of us are regular people who, on any given day, find ourselves somewhere along the continuum between unquenchable optimism and inconsolable despair, but generally not at either extreme. Faced with the seemingly inscrutable nature of hope, it seems reasonable to adopt a philosophy very similar to the one expressed by Miss Lavender Lewis, a character in Lucy Maud Montgomery's *Anne of Avonlea*: "In this world you've just got to hope for the best and prepare for the worst and take whatever God sends."[20]

Rather than trying to make sense of all these confusing ideas, perhaps a better choice is to pragmatically accept the notion that life will give us our fair share of sour grapes, and that if we keep eating them, we can expect to eventually find some sweet ones, which clear the bitterness of the others from our palate. Perhaps we should just acknowledge the futility of the exercise and abandon any effort to unravel the definitions and nuances of hope, as well as any sense of urgency to do so.

That's a perfectly acceptable way to live—until it's not.

Until airplanes crash into skyscrapers and war breaks out. Until the stock market plummets and your life savings become worthless. Until the family business goes bankrupt. Until a car accident severs a limb or leaves a loved one unable to care for themselves. Until the cancer diagnosis arrives with a prognosis of six weeks to live. Until you can't find work for a year and a half. Until you miscarry, then again, then again, and again. Until you deplete your life savings on in vitro fertilization without success. Until your daughter commits suicide. Until your spouse cheats on you. Until your teenage son runs away from home and goes missing for six months. Until your identity is stolen and your credit is ruined. Until your best friend dies unexpectedly.

It is in those moments, and a million others like them, that you abruptly realize that chasing desires with a hint of *que será será* will not suffice. When you're trying to hold the few strands of sanity you have left as tightly as you can, wishing things were different serves no use. When you're hanging off the end of your rope, being told that what doesn't kill you makes you stronger does nothing to stop your weary grip from slipping. Singing that the sun will come out tomorrow is

Understanding Hope

pointless when you're afraid you won't make it through the night. When faced with unavoidable realities like old age, declining health, and death, trying to find a pathway around them is futile.

It is in those moments, and a million others like them, that you need hope—not the kind you buy with a penny at a wishing well, or the kind that asks you to pull yourself up by your own bootstraps. You need genuine, life-changing hope from outside yourself that proves itself when it matters most; hope that reliably and consistently points you in the right direction; hope that answers questions, not creates more. It needs to be real. It needs to make a difference. It needs to work—every time, everywhere, in every situation, without fail. If it doesn't, it's not even worth a penny tossed into a well.

I knew from the beginning that the Bible is the only place to find that kind of hope. I turned to dictionaries and psychological studies because I believe all truth is God's truth. I thought I might find a consistent thread among these different perspectives that could clue me in on where I had gone wrong. I did, but not in the way I expected. To my shock and dismay, I discovered that I had bought into all of these different philosophies—some more than others—but all more than I should have. I had no idea how much I had allowed these inconsistent and flawed concepts to permeate my thinking. Even though I still couldn't clearly articulate what the biblical definition of hope was, I recognized that none of these, or any combination of them, would withstand the test of waiting in the real world. The weight I was carrying was proof of that.

The biblical definition of hope

So, I broke out my Bible and study tools and started searching for a biblical definition of hope, and I found it. It's rooted in Hebrews 11:1.

Although this verse directly provides us with the definition of faith, it also indirectly defines hope. In the King James Version (KJV), Hebrews 11:1 reads as follows:

> Now faith is the substance of things hoped for, the evidence of things not seen.

Despite writing in Greek, the author of Hebrews is speaking to a Jewish audience. Throughout the book, he illustrates his points using the ancient Hebrew Scriptures, known today as the Old Testament. His arguments often employ rhetorical techniques found in Old Testament writings and commonly used by Jewish rabbis in their schools. Hebrews 11:1 is framed in a literary structure of Hebrew poetry called synonymous parallelism, where the same concept is expressed twice in different words to expand and enhance its meaning. The goal is not to establish a precise equivalence between the two statements but rather for them to complement each other, with one adding color or nuance to the other.

In this case, the parallelism is easy to identify. "Faith" is clearly the main concept defined by the two parallel phrases. The words "substance" and "evidence" are parallel to one another, as are the phrases "things hoped for" and "things not seen."

At first blush, this does not seem to help us much with defining hope. In fact, if we simply equate "hope" to "not seen" we end up with a concept of hope that is similar to Aristotle's. Aristotle thought that "hope is a waking dream,"[21] meaning that it is nothing more than anticipation. Dreams can be good, or they can be nightmares, but either way they're not real. To Aristotle, the only difference between hope and a dream was whether your eyes were open or not. The result of this reasoning is that hope becomes whatever you envision it to be. If you hope for good things, good things happen; if you anticipate bad things, that's what you get. It's a very fatalistic, egocentric, make-your-own-truth philosophy of life—not a perspective consistent with the whole teaching of the Bible or with the illustrations of faith and hope the author of Hebrews cites in the remainder of chapter 11 and into chapter 12. Therefore, there must be more to hope being unseen than what meets the eye, if you'll pardon the pun.

While it is undisputable that hope involves unseen things, the exact nature of these things and their relationship to hope can't be deduced simply from a literary construct. For more insight, we must examine the surrounding context.

In the passages leading up to chapter 11, the author explains how Jesus fulfilled all the sacrificial requirements of the old Mosaic covenant and became the mediator of a new covenant, in which we no longer need to offer daily sacrifices for the forgiveness of sins because "we have been sanctified through the offering of the body of Jesus Christ once for all . . . For by one offering He has perfected for all time those who are sanctified" (Hebrews 10:10, 14). Based on this perfect and permanent forgiveness, and the confidence it provides, he urges his readers to do three things: "draw near with a sincere heart in full assurance of faith", "hold fast the confession of our hope without wavering," and "consider how to stimulate one another to love and good deeds" (Hebrews 10:22-24). These exhortations were necessary because they were enduring "a great conflict of suffering" (Hebrews 10:32). He encourages them:

> Therefore, do not throw away your confidence, which has a great reward. For you have need of endurance, so that when you have done the will of God, you may receive what was promised.

FOR YET IN A VERY LITTLE WHILE,
HE WHO IS COMING WILL COME, AND WILL NOT DELAY.
BUT MY RIGHTEOUS ONE SHALL LIVE BY FAITH;
AND IF HE SHRINKS BACK, MY SOUL HAS NO PLEASURE IN HIM.

But we are not of those who shrink back to destruction, but of those who have faith to the preserving of the soul. (Hebrews 10:35-39)

Notice the repeated themes in the last 11 verses of chapter 10: faith, hope, confidence, and endurance. These people had started out believing that Jesus' sacrifice paid for their sins and that He was the Messiah for whom they and their ancestors had hoped for centuries, willingly and gladly accepting the persecution that accompanied it. However, a long time had passed, and the persecution had not eased. It was wearing them down, and they were starting to doubt whether the ridicule and suffering they endured at the hands of both the Romans and the unbelieving Jewish community was worth it. They were tempted to revert to their old ways, to worship in the synagogues as they had before, because at least then, they would no longer be ostracized by their family and community. The author encourages them to cling to what they have believed because it is true and grounded in God's promises found in the Scriptures. The new covenant is not merely the better of two good options; it's the only one that counts because the new has replaced the old. Although a lot of the same terminology is used and the new covenant shares the same foundation as the old, the differences matter because the sacrifices under the Law of Moses were never intended to be the permanent solution to sin.

Quoting Habakkuk 2:3-4, he reminds them that the righteous live by faith and then goes on to remind them what faith is and what it looks like, starting with the verse on which we're currently focused.

Against this backdrop, we see two things about hope as we reach Hebrews 11:1. The first is that hope is a fundamental component of faith. Hope serves to define faith, rather than the opposite. While they are closely linked, they are not identical. In fact, faith is evidently reliant on hope in some manner, even if we have not yet determined the specifics, to the extent that it seems reasonable to conclude that faith cannot exist without hope. The second is that faith enhances hope by adding "substance" and "evidence." You begin with hope, whatever that entails; and when you incorporate substance or evidence into it, or when you produce substance or evidence of it, you establish faith. Now, let's examine "substance" and "evidence" more closely to discover how they can help us.

The Greek word translated "substance" in the KJV is *hupostasis*, a compound word consisting of a preposition meaning "under" and a verb that means "to make or cause to stand up." The imagery is unmistakable. In concrete terms, it represents a support, a brace, or an underpinning that holds up something else. In abstract contexts, it describes a proof that makes an idea or argument to withstand scrutiny or critique. Our English word "substance" is derived from a Latin preposition and verb combination that mean exactly what the corresponding Greek terms do, making "substance" a direct and literal translation of *hupostasis*.

The Greek word for "evidence" is *elegchos*. In logical and rhetorical contexts, it means "proof"; in legal and moral contexts, it means "conviction" or "a reproof, correction, or censure of something wrong." In its verb form, it means "to bring something to light; to demonstrate, prove, or disprove something; to convince." At its core is the idea of calling out the truth and establishing it as fact.

With this understanding, the definition of faith takes shape. Faith is concrete action based on something abstract. It is proof that you believe in something that cannot be empirically proven. It demonstrates that you are convinced of a reality that cannot be seen.

This is precisely the thesis of Hebrews 11, in which the author cites numerous examples of people who, by faith, did something concrete because they were convinced of the reality and truth of things that could not be independently verified. Based on the unseen, they willingly attempted feats, accepted challenges, and endured hardships that no rational person would even contemplate—unless they were equally convinced of the same unseen reality. After providing example after example of people evidencing their hope, even in the face of horrific consequences, he delivers his punch line in Hebrews 12:1: don't lose hope. Instead, recognize that the testimonies of these individuals prove that the unseen things on which they based their actions are indeed real and true, and fix your eyes on Jesus, the ultimate example of faith, "who for the joy set before Him (hope) endured the cross (faith), despising the shame, and sat down at the right hand of God" (Hebrews 12:2).

Now that we have a solid idea of what faith is, we can use the relationship between faith and hope to understand what hope is. To do this, we're going to use another form of parallelism. Instead of comparing two phrases in a single sentence, we will compare two translations of the same verse. As we have noted, the KJV translates Hebrews 11:1 as:

> Now faith is the substance of things hoped for, the evidence of things not seen.

The New American Standard Bible (NASB) words it a bit differently:

> Now faith is the assurance of things hoped for, the conviction of things not seen.

Although assurance and conviction appear quite different from substance and evidence in English, we have already seen that they are legitimate translations of the Greek words *hupostasis* and *elegchos*, respectively. Interestingly, the words used in the KJV are concrete and emphasize action, while those used in the NASB are abstract and emphasize motivation. Both aspects are valid concepts inherent in the original words and represent two sides of the same coin. As a result, the KJV conveys more about what faith is, while the NASB offers deeper insight into what hope is, without detracting from each other. We demonstrate our assurance of things hoped for in tangible ways, and our actions reveal our conviction of things not seen. When we have hope, we exercise faith; when we exercise faith, we do so based on hope. So, what is biblical hope? It is the confident conviction of an unseen reality that causes us to act. The conviction is hope; the action is faith.

This resonates even more strongly in Hebrews 10, where the author emphasizes confidence, full assurance, and holding fast. Hope is confidence, not wishful thinking; it is a reality of which you can be fully assured, not just a possibility or even a probability; it is something tangible you hold on to, even if you can't see it.

Comparing definitions

We can now see how biblical hope is radically different from any other definition we've examined. It is not wishful thinking because, although the things we wish for are unseen, they are not things we are confident exist by definition. We want them to be true, but there's a chance they aren't. The premise of a philosophy based on wishful thinking is that if I want it badly enough, wish for it hard enough, and believe in it fervently enough, I can make it true. In contrast, biblical hope instead says I believe it, want it, and act on it because it is already true.

Believing based on rational expectation also isn't biblical hope. This isn't to say that biblical hope and faith are irrational or nonsensical. On the contrary, hope and faith are very rational and logically consistent. The difference is that The Beatles had confidence in the sun coming up tomorrow because they had witnessed it happen before, leading them to reasonably expect it would happen again. In other words, rational expectation assumes that seeing is believing. Biblical hope, however, is grounded in truths that must be accepted as axiomatic without empirical proof, because they are not just unseen but unseeable. In other words, biblical hope posits that believing is seeing.

While "believing is seeing" may sound like something you might find on the inside flap of a book about positive thinking, biblical hope is not the same as positive thinking. The distinction between the two lies in the nature and origin of the unseen things we believe in. Inherent in the positivity school of thought is the notion that I can create my own unseen reality, as advocated by Irene Cara. This notion is expressed in the poem *"Invictus,"* which claims, "I am the master of my fate; I am the captain of my soul."[22] Although this perspective on hope may be more brash in its expression, it ultimately amounts to nothing more than wishful thinking amped up on the steroids of self-confidence and determination. Conversely, the confidence and assurance of biblical hope do not come from oneself. In fact, prior to chapter 11, the author of Hebrews has painstakingly established that only Jesus Himself can be a sufficient sacrifice for the forgiveness of sins and warns of the terrifying consequences for anyone who attempts to stand outside of that grace. You are visible; so hope based on your ability to control your own destiny isn't biblical hope because it is based on you, while biblical hope is rooted in confidence in things that are not seen. In other words, we believe in the unseen things because they are real—they do not become real simply because we believe in them.

It's hard to argue that the single mom in Whitney Houston's song, *"Never Give Up,"* who works two jobs just to feed her child, isn't focusing on an unseen reality. She's pushing through challenges that sound very similar to the things the people listed in Hebrews 11 endured. Her belief that things will eventually improve drives her to keep moving forward, which sounds like faith. However, where this philosophy breaks down is when we realize that her belief is only valid and is only going to work as long as she never, ever, ever gives up. Put simply, this is having faith in faith. Believing for the sake of believing or having faith in anything as long as you have faith, isn't biblical hope. For that kind of hope to work, the unseen reality would need to be faith itself, meaning that faith and hope are synonymous. However, as we've shown, biblical faith and hope are not synonymous. Faith is a concrete action rooted in conviction in an unseen reality, which means that faith itself cannot be that unseen reality. Any attempt to argue otherwise quickly devolves into a spiral of circular reasoning that essentially amounts to belief in oneself, which, as we have just seen is not consistent with a biblical understanding of hope. From a biblical perspective, while the determination, persistence, and fortitude displayed by Whitney's single mom are admirable and can signify genuine hope, they cannot serve as the foundation of her hope.

Finally, Dr. Snyder's and the psychological community's concept of goal-based hope is not biblical hope either. Several of the fallacies we've already discussed apply to Snyder's theory as well, but it's worth highlighting that the very idea of pathways thinking makes it inconsistent with biblical hope. Biblical hope isn't something that can be reached by multiple paths. It is absolute and binary: you either believe that the unseen things are true, or you don't. There is no "hope scale" where you can be somewhat hopeful or mostly hopeful about the unseen realities that the Bible claims to be true: you either have confidence in them, or you don't. Dr. Snyder's system offers interesting and useful insights into goal-oriented thinking and behavior, but it does not come close to capturing biblical hope.

You may be starting to realize at this point that the reason our hopes are so easily dashed is that they are built on either things we see, things that are not real, or things we are not convinced of. If I say to you, "I hope you feel better," it is a genuine expression of what I wish to be true. However, even if you are merely suffering from a common cold, I have no way of knowing that you will recover, no substantive means of guaranteeing that outcome, and certainly no intention of wagering a year's salary on it. It's perfectly fine to use the word "hope" in a colloquial sense to express our desire for something to happen of which we are unsure, such as hoping for someone to recover from an illness, hoping to land that promotion or new job, or hoping that our team wins the championship. There are many examples in Scripture where godly men and women used it in exactly that way. The challenge comes when we realize that hope is part of the glue meant to hold our lives together and help us make sense of the difficulties we face. If we can't distinguish between a colloquial expression of uncertainty and a cornerstone of our worldview that drives how we view and interpret life, confusion and disillusionment become inevitable.

To move past that confusion, we can't just leave our understanding of hope as "confidence in unseen things" because there are many things we can't see. The author of Hebrews references "things that are not seen" a couple of times in chapter 11, but he does not clarify what they are, as he assumes they are self-evident. If you're like me, however, you probably prefer a bit more specificity. Let's see if we can find some.

Chapter Two
Redefining Good

God is our hope

Even though we have established that hope is confidence in an unseen reality, we still have more work to do to fully articulate this definition. What exactly is this unseen reality, and if it is unseen, how can we know it is real?

The answer to the first question is fairly straightforward. Out of the 73 instances where the word "hope" appears in the NASB, more than one-third reference God Himself as our hope, whether it's an author claiming Him as his hope or exhorting someone to place their hope in God. Below are a few representative examples:

> For You are my hope; O Lord GOD, You are my confidence from my youth. (Psalm 71:5)

> Why are you in despair, O my soul? And why have you become disturbed within me? Hope in God, for I shall yet praise Him, The help of my countenance and my God. (Psalm 42:11)

O LORD, the hope of Israel, All who forsake You will be put to shame. Those who turn away on earth will be written down, Because they have forsaken the fountain of living water, even the LORD. (Jeremiah 17:13)

But this I admit to you, that according to the Way which they call a sect I do serve the God of our fathers, believing everything that is in accordance with the Law and that is written in the Prophets; having a hope in God, which these men cherish themselves, that there shall certainly be a resurrection of both the righteous and the wicked. (Acts 24:14-15)

Now may the God of hope fill you with all joy and peace in believing, so that you will abound in hope by the power of the Holy Spirit. (Romans 15:13)

If we have hoped in Christ in this life only, we are of all men most to be pitied. (1 Corinthians 15:19)

These references to God as our hope do not include other things the Bible says we hope in, which are dependent upon God Himself, such as His name, His mercy, His faithfulness, His word, redemption from sin, and His future return to earth. Some of these things have not yet been manifested, while others have. Some have been partially realized, and several are inherently intangible. However, none of them hold any weight or validity if God is not real and is not as the Bible describes Him.

The unseen, the real, and the good

God is certainly unseen. The Apostle John states this clearly on two occasions: once in his gospel (John 1:8) and again in his epistles

(1 John 4:12). Even most of those who doubt or deny God's existence would likely agree that if He does exist, He is invisible. In fact, for many, the inability to see God is often a key reason they find it challenging to believe in His existence. This brings us to the second part of our working definition of hope. If God is to be our hope, He must not only be unseen, but He must also be real.

I recognize that you may not believe God is real. Perhaps you accept the concept of God because that's what you were taught when you were young, but feel He abandoned you when you needed Him most. Maybe you're inspired to believe things will get better when you read verses like, "Why are you in despair, O my soul? And why have you become disturbed within me? Hope in God, for I shall again praise Him for the help of His presence" (Psalm 42:5). Yet, despite this encouragement, the despair soon returns, God feels far away, and you're left wondering how any of this is supposed to have any lasting benefit.

Ironically, the disillusionment many people cite as their reason for not believing in God illustrates how closely hope is tied to the reality of God. It's as if we instinctively know that if God is real, so is hope, and that if we doubt or deny His existence, sustaining hope becomes impossible.

However, merely accepting the premise that God exists doesn't answer all the questions and confusion surrounding hope. I do believe that God is real, but as I struggled with my wife's diagnosis, my soul remained troubled within me. When Greg's caring inquiry was all it took to pierce my facade of peace and joy, I was forced to admit that the psalmist was connecting the existence of God to hope in a way I hadn't grasped. I needed to look further.

Fortunately, I didn't have to look very far. The foundation for connecting the existence of God to hope is found, interestingly, just a few verses after the definitions of faith and hope in Hebrews 11. In verse 6, we read:

> he who comes to God must believe that He is and that He is a rewarder of those who seek Him.

If I want to come to God, I must believe He exists. If I don't believe He exists, why would I want to come to Him? That sounds reasonable enough. However, the author adds something else—something he considers just as basic, foundational, and obvious as the idea that only those who believe God exists would come to Him: that He rewards those who seek Him. Suddenly, I saw the connection. Hope is based not only on believing in God's existence but also on trusting in His character.

I don't believe it is an accident that these two truths are introduced as foundational and axiomatic in the initial chapter of Genesis. We find the first in the opening statement of the book: "In the beginning, God . . ." We are given no defense, no rationale, and no justification for God's existence—it is simply assumed as obvious and true.

The second isn't as blatant, but it's there, nonetheless. To believe that God rewards those who seek Him is to believe something about His character; and the very first thing that is established about God's character is that He is good. Seven times in Genesis 1, we are told that everything God created was good, with the seventh emphasizing that it was all very good. Isn't it remarkable that out of all the attributes of God the first one we encounter is His goodness? Before we learn anything about holiness, judgment, grace, mercy, truth, or even love, we are told He is good. Is goodness not what comes to mind when you think of God rewarding those who seek Him? Or, perhaps more to the point, when you feel He's not rewarding you for seeking Him, don't you question His goodness? I do.

In other words, the implication of Hebrews 11:6 is that hope requires that you believe God is good.

Questioning the goodness of God is as old as time itself. When the serpent deceived Eve in Genesis 3, he didn't challenge God's existence or any of His other attributes—he questioned His goodness. "God didn't tell you the truth," he hissed. "You're not going to die. He doesn't want you to eat that fruit because He knows that if you do, you will be like Him. He doesn't want to reward you; He's holding out on you." Both Eve and Adam fell for that lie, doubting the goodness of God, and all mankind has been doubting it ever since.

It seems counterintuitive that those who believe God exists would not also believe He is good, but belief in the goodness of God is not as certain as one might think. Even those who assert it confidently one day can often be found feeling angry at God and blaming Him for their life circumstances the next. Especially in the face of hardship, challenging situations, and bad outcomes, the goodness of God is debated as much, if not more than, His existence. For many, both atheists and theists alike, questions such as, "Why do bad things happen to good people?" present significant hurdles. For atheists, the presence of evil in the world serves as proof that God does not exist; for theists, it is a reason to doubt that God is truly good.

Jesus touched upon this dynamic in the Sermon on the Mount. In Matthew 7:11, addressing our hesitancy to pray, He says, "If you then, being evil, know how to give good gifts to your children, how much more will your Father who is in heaven give what is good to those who ask Him!" We don't ask God for things because in our heart of hearts we don't believe He's good enough to give them to us. When we do ask and don't receive what we ask for, we quickly assume that He's not good, because if He were, He would have given us what we wanted when we wanted it.

Do you see how relevant this is to the concept of hope? I may claim that God is my hope, but when circumstances don't turn out as I expect them to or wish they would, my confidence in God's goodness wanes, and my hope along with it.

Thankful for flat tires

I never realized how much I had fallen victim to this fallacy until the Lord brought me through an eye-opening, heart-transforming spiritual awakening that began—as I'm sure most of your life-changing spiritual encounters have—with a flat tire. My wife was taking one of our sons to a couple of doctor appointments we had worked hard to coordinate and schedule together. She had all of our children with her, except for my oldest daughter who was at work. The only vehicles we had access to at the time were the minivan my wife was driving and my daughter's car. When my wife called me to report the flat, I was at home by myself working on a highly visible and time-sensitive project I was struggling to finish.

As she gave me her location, all I could think about was that I had let our auto club membership expire just two weeks earlier to save on household expenses. I tried, unsuccessfully, to conceal my frustration as I told her I would try to figure something out before hanging up the phone. I remember muttering something to myself about how incredibly bad timing this was. Little did I realize that God was about to use this interruption in my day to completely disrupt my perspective on good and bad and change my life forever.

My daughter could only leave work for a short time, so she picked me up, took me to the stranded minivan, and then returned to her job. The van was relatively new, so I had never changed a tire on it before; however, I wasn't exactly a tire-changing rookie, so I wasn't particularly concerned. As it turned out, I horribly underestimated the challenge. When I got to the disabled vehicle, I found that the spare was underneath the car, between the two front seats—not an easy place to get to.

After searching for about 15 minutes for the hidden bolt I needed to turn to winch the spare down to the ground, I discovered that the tools provided by the car manufacturer were not adequate to lower the spare easily, making it awkward, time-consuming, and frustrating. Once I had finally retrieved the spare, jacked the car up, and removed the lug nuts, I discovered, to my dismay, that I could not get the flat tire to break free from the wheel.

I pulled, pushed, hit it with my fist, and kicked it with my feet. I shook it as hard as I dared without knocking the car off the jack, but the old tire would not budge. I called a few people for advice, and they all told me to do the same things I had already tried. Eventually, I broke down and called the auto club to renew my membership because I figured the only way this tire was coming off was at a shop, so I needed a tow. The auto club told me the nearest guy was about 40 minutes away. What had originally been inconvenient was now downright annoying.

As I sat waiting for the tow truck, the Holy Spirit prompted me, "In everything give thanks; for this is the will of God in Christ Jesus concerning you" (I Thessalonians 5:18). I chuckled to myself at the simplicity of this spiritual exercise. "Why not?" I said to myself. I certainly had nothing better to do while I waited.

So, I began to identify the silver lining to my inconvenient black cloud. The flat occurred while my wife was pulling away from a stoplight, so she wasn't going very fast. It was a rear tire that blew, not a front tire, so she didn't lose control of the vehicle. The road she was on was extremely busy and had no shoulder, but she managed to pull onto a little side street where a strip mall was under development, which meant we were safe from passing traffic and I had plenty of room to wrestle with the flat.

We were within walking distance of a 24-hour convenience store, so we had access to drinks and restrooms while we waited. It was a gorgeous spring day in Texas—not too humid, not too hot—a bona fide miracle in and of itself. My wife was able to reschedule the missed doctor's appointments. The new auto club membership I purchased was significantly less expensive than the one I had let lapse. It came with only a 3-mile towing benefit, but the nearest tire store was only 1.5 miles away. I had plenty to be thankful for.

But that's not what the Lord was getting at. "Anybody can be thankful for the silver lining," He chided. "Anyone can be grateful that the situation wasn't as serious as it could have been. What I'm asking is if you're thankful for the flat tire itself."

Really? How do you even manage that? Wasn't it enough that I could see grace in a tough situation? Was it really fair to expect me to actually be thankful for the bad thing that happened, as if it were something good? Was I not entitled to be unhappy when bad things occur? I should have at least been allowed to be annoyed. After all, I may have had to lump it, but I didn't have to like it—right?

Somehow, I sensed that it wasn't quite as simple as that, or rather, He wasn't going to let me dismiss the question that easily. As I sat chewing on that conundrum, the tow driver finally showed up, only he wasn't driving a tow truck. Instead, he had a small Toyota half-ton pickup, with no equipment to tow anything. "Great! This just keeps getting better," I thought to myself.

I knew he wasn't going to help me get the tow truck I obviously needed unless I let him give it the old college try (or, in this guy's case, probably the old I-may-not-have-even-finished-high-school try), so I didn't say anything. He walked over to the jacked-up wheel and banged on it with his fists. "Good luck, fella," I smirked to myself. Then he kicked it a couple of times. Gee, why hadn't I thought of that? He turned away from the car, and I thought, "Good. Now he'll get on the phone, call a real tow driver, and maybe I'll get home before dark." But instead of reaching for a phone, he picked up the spare tire and slung it against the frozen wheel. Whack! on one side, then Whack! on the other, and the flat fell off like a coffee-soaked donut.

I hadn't felt that foolish or embarrassed in a long time. My only saving grace was that I hadn't actually verbalized any of my disdainful remarks to the repairman. That really didn't matter much, though, because God certainly heard them all. The weird thing was that, once again, He wasn't driving home the obvious point. "Yeah, yeah, yeah," He said to me. "You're arrogant, you're foolish, you're rude. You've been humbled, and it smarts, but you'll get over it. What I want to know is: are you thankful for the flat tire?"

Huh? This isn't about me needing to be put in my place and reminded that I am completely dependent on Him? "You still want me to be thankful for the flat tire? What does that even mean? How am I supposed to do that?" His silence told me I had stumbled upon the $64,000 question, but He didn't provide any further clarification. It was as if He considered the solution was as obvious as using the spare to knock the flat free from the wheel, and that I was just as clueless about the one as I had been about the other. I had no idea how to be grateful for something bad.

He let me stew on the question for several weeks, but I got nowhere. I even talked to a couple of smart, godly people about this. They acknowledged the legitimacy of the problem statement, yet they were scratching their heads just as much as I was. Eventually, I recognized that there was indeed a difference between being thankful for the silver lining and being thankful for the black cloud itself, but I still had no clue how to do the latter. I also realized that if I ever wanted to be thankful for the "bad" stuff, and not just be content to be thankful for the "good," I would need to adopt a perspective that would revolutionize my life, so I kept working on it. No matter how hard I tried, however, I couldn't find any line of reasoning that made sense, and it truly began to bother me.

Affliction is good

I guess the Lord must have eventually determined that I had wallowed in this long enough, or perhaps He just grew tired of waiting for me to get there on my own. Either way, He finally revealed the key to me. Hidden in the middle of Psalm 119 are these very enlightening words:

> Before I was afflicted I went astray,
> But now I keep Your word.
> You are good and do good;
> Teach me Your statutes.
> The arrogant have forged a lie against me;
> With all my heart I will observe Your precepts.
> Their heart is covered with fat,
> But I delight in Your law.
> It is good for me that I was afflicted,
> That I may learn Your statutes. (Psalm 119:67-71)

I reeled at verse 71. *Affliction is good? What kind of sadomasochistic nonsense is this?* Taking another look, I saw that the psalmist isn't rejoicing or taking pleasure in the pain itself, nor does he imply that God enjoys inflicting it. Instead, he views his affliction as good and valuable because it teaches him how to keep God's word. Testing, challenges, affliction, and all other forms of adversity are good because they clarify where we are mature and where we still need to grow. We would keep going astray unless we were called back to keeping God's word—and affliction does that for us. It keeps us running towards the safety of obedience instead of chasing the lie of self-sufficiency. That is not only something for which we should be very grateful; it's also the manifestation of hope.

"Good" and "bad" are relative terms and concepts that only hold meaning when a standard is established. The law of God, as communicated in His word, represents His perfect and holy nature—the ultimate standard by which all other standards are judged. When I prioritize His holiness in my life above everything else, everything He does in my life is good. From that perspective, there is no such thing as a "bad" experience, because I see it all as contributing to the holiness of God in my life.

That's a particularly difficult perspective to maintain because some of the things that can and do happen to us are genuinely horrific in nature. In no way am I denying the reality of unadulterated evil in the world or suggesting that we call things like rape, murder, abuse, sexual immorality, lying, stealing, or any other sin "good." God certainly does not call those things good, and neither should we. However, I tend to have a very egotistical view of good and bad, which leads me to assign those labels based on whether I like them, rather than their intrinsic moral value. I generally take a self-centered approach to genuine sin, justifying my own actions and expressing outrage at those of others based on my opinions of them and not on what God thinks.

That being said, there is also a vast category of things that have no intrinsic moral designation—things that are not inherently good or bad but are described as such based on preference and perspective.

Affliction falls into this category. I doubt anyone views being beaten as a positive experience, but the Bible states that after John and Peter were flogged for speaking in the name of Jesus, they left "rejoicing that they had been considered worthy to suffer shame for His name" (Acts 5:41).

Paul, who was flogged five times, beaten with rods three times, stoned, shipwrecked, adrift at sea for 24 hours, and falsely accused and imprisoned multiple times (2 Corinthians 11: 24-27), wrote during one of those imprisonments that he rejoiced that the gospel was being preached, even if it was being done maliciously to try to cause him more harm (Philippians 1:16-18). The author of Hebrews says that Jesus endured the cross because of the joy set before Him (Hebrews 12:2), and Jesus Himself told us to love our enemies, and to pray for and do good to those who mistreat us (Matthew 5:39-43). Clearly, all of these men had a different understanding of affliction than many of us do.

God is good because that's all He can be

I don't think it is merely coincidental that the psalmist specifically addresses affliction in the context of God's goodness. Of all the things that make me question God's goodness, affliction is at the top of the list. Whether it's something as trivial as a flat tire or as life-altering as chronic pain, nothing challenges my belief in God's goodness—and therefore my hope—more than affliction.

Affliction creates the context in which I feel the weight of the wait most acutely. My mind, my heart, and my body scream out for relief. The little annoyances of everyday life pile up. Then, major trauma strikes, delivering bone-crunching, soul-crushing blows. Forget about winning; I just want it to be over. "If God is truly good," I tell myself, "surely He will intervene and put an end to the pain." Every passing second that He doesn't seems only to add insult to injury. Therefore, if I can understand affliction from God's perspective, dealing with other things which are neither intrinsically good nor bad will become much easier. As radical a shift in our thinking as this requires, the psalmist's approach to answering the problem of affliction is amazingly simple:

> You are good and do good;
> Teach me Your statutes. (Psalm 119:68)

This isn't just a chorus from a children's Sunday School song or a saying on an inspirational poster; it is a core theological tenet of the Christian faith. Our God is not like the capricious gods of the Greeks or Romans, who were modeled after the foibles of humanity. God is good because that is all He can be. If He were anything else but good, He wouldn't be God. It is inherent to His nature. If any part of His character is bad, He ceases to be God. Consequently, God does good because that is all He can do. Doing good is mandated by His nature. If He would do a single bad act, He would cease to be God. He must be good and do good, or He is not God. Likewise, He cannot be bad or do bad, not even once, or He is not God. He is good, and He does good. Period. Any concept, logic, or reasoning that denies this to any degree or in any fashion is false.

As a result, God is the only unseen entity in which we can have absolute confidence, making Him the only solid foundation for hope. Thus, we can refine our definition of hope from "confidence in an unseen reality" to "confidence in the goodness of God," because all genuine unseen realities stem from God Himself, and anything that originates from Him must be good, as He is good because that's all He can be, and He does good because that's all He can do.

Note that the psalmist pairs the assertion of God's goodness with a prayer to be taught God's "statutes." Statutes are edicts prescribed or decreed by a governing authority. They are not debated or negotiated, nor are they put to a referendum or a vote. They are recognized as true and valid simply because they are declared to be so.

Practically speaking, this means that when He brings blessings and wealth into my life, He does so because He is good. When He brings discipline and chastening into my life, He does so because He is good. When He introduces disease and pestilence into my life, He does so because He is good. When I get angry with Him for what He brings into my life and call it "bad", I am essentially substituting my definition of good for His, replacing His standard with my own. This is why the psalmist realized he needed to be taught differently. Since all He does is good, when I label it "bad," I am essentially calling Him "bad." If I truly believe that God is good, I must accept *everything* from His hand as good. This is difficult because I don't have the same perspective He does to understand that it is all good. As a result, when faced with things I dislike, I not only need to trust that He is good, but I also have to learn to view them the same way He does, adjusting my definition of good to match His.

Equally important, when I encounter genuine evil, I can be absolutely assured that He did not cause it. It may stem from the presence of sin and its effects in the world, it may arise from the evil in men's hearts, or it may even be a direct act of the devil and his minions, but it absolutely, unequivocally, and undeniably did not come from the hand of God. Whether it is as trivial as a flat tire or as significant as the death of a loved one, if He caused it, it's good; if it's truly bad, He didn't cause it.

If hope is so clear-cut and the goodness of God is so undeniable, why do I struggle so much with being hopeful? Generally, I do not question God's power or right to do as He wants, but I do question His motives—much like the serpent convinced Eve to do in the Garden of Eden. Ultimately, it boils down to a question of control. If you revisit the human definitions of hope we discussed earlier, you'll notice that they are all egocentric: my wish, my reasonable expectation, my passion, my bootstraps, my goals, and how I'm going to make them reality. However, if I place my hope in God, I must surrender all those things to Him and trust that the choices He makes will be better than the ones I would make, which immediately puts His goodness in question.

Spencer Te'o's testimony

I recently heard a testimony of this dynamic playing out in real life. Former Pittsburgh Steelers quarterback Ben Roethlisberger hosts a podcast called *Footbahlin,* where he discusses football—primarily Steelers football—but also shares insights about his faith, fatherhood, as well as whatever may be of interest for athletes and other personalities that appear as guests. The idea is for him to sit around and chat with his friend, producer, and co-host, Spencer Te'o, nicknamed Spence, just like guys do while watching a game together and talking about life. In early 2024, the popular weekly podcast ended abruptly, without any announcement or explanation, catching Ben's extensive YouTube viewership by surprise. About seven months later, Ben and Spence released a new episode where they clarified the reasons behind their mysterious absence.

In the summer of 2023, Spence and his wife learned they were expecting their second child, a girl. During the 20-week ultrasound, they received some disturbing news: their little unborn baby girl had a problem with her kidneys. It was uncertain whether there was a cyst in her kidneys or if they were simply not functioning, but the situation was serious. Moreover, one of her femurs was significantly underdeveloped, and her nasal bone was absent—both possible indicators of Down syndrome. If the child managed to survive the pregnancy, the outlook afterward was not very optimistic.

Shortly after the podcast that turned out to be the last one before the unplanned hiatus, Spence's wife was rushed to the hospital for an emergency C-section, and the child was immediately admitted to the Neonatal Intensive Care Unit. Fortunately, her bones had developed normally, and there was no evidence of Down syndrome, but she faced new life-threatening complications. She had to be intubated because she could not breathe on her own and required the most advanced ventilator available due to her small size and the severity of her condition. Chest tubes were inserted to drain air that was escaping through holes in her lungs. Even more concerning was the air pocket forming in her abdomen, indicating a hole in her intestine, which, if not repaired quickly, could lead to infection and sepsis.

The challenge was that the hospital where she was born was not adequately equipped to perform that kind of surgery on an infant. There was a children's hospital about a mile away where the surgery could be performed, but doctors feared that if they transferred her to a less advanced ventilator, which would be necessary for transporting her to the children's hospital, she might not survive the trip; and if she did, she likely would not survive the surgery itself. The unspoken pressure from the medical staff was for Spence and his wife to prepare for the reality that their daughter would inevitably die.

Nothing could be more devastating and draining of hope than for a set of parents to face such an impossible decision. It was a burden that Spence, as the father, felt very intensely. He admits to buckling under the pressure of deciding whether to do nothing and watch his little girl die or to move her and undergo surgery that could also lead to her death. Either way, he would be responsible for his daughter's death—a daughter that neither he nor his wife had yet been able to hold due to the machines keeping her alive.

Both the Te'os and Roethlisbergers profess faith in Christ, so they and their entire church family rallied together for mutual support and prayer. What was only three or four days on the clock seemed like three or four lifetimes. The constant requests for updates from worried friends and family only highlighted the complete lack of answers. Spence finally decided to take the risk and travel to the children's hospital. As the ventilator and other machines were disconnected, the little girl began to breathe on her own, and instead of declining, her numbers improved. She survived the one-mile journey, but the miracles didn't end there.

Once they got her into the operating room, the surgeons examined her bowels in search of the hole that needed repair, but they found none—it was completely healed. Spence mentions that when the nurse practitioner came from the operating room to talk to them, she looked as white as a ghost, and they feared the worst. When she reported, incredulously, that the hole was no longer there, Spence's wife smiled at the nurse and said, "I don't know if you're a Christian, but you're about to be!" At the time of the podcast in which Spence shared this story, his daughter was doing extremely well. He confirmed she would eventually need a kidney transplant, but the immediate danger had passed.

As Spence related his story, he mentioned that when he first learned of his daughter's condition at the 20-week ultrasound, he prayed and felt God reassuring him that she would be fine. He wasn't entirely sure what that meant, but when they learned that Down syndrome was no longer a risk, he assumed that was the case, little knowing the additional miraculous interventions he would witness. When he shared that confidence with a friend, they asked, "How did you know it was God who told you that?" His answer, which I've transcribed below from the podcast with minor edits for clarity, is very insightful.

> There are two answers to that, that I've come to realize at this point. The theological answer is that the more time you spend with God, the more familiar with His voice you become. The practical answer is that I didn't know it was God's. I believed it to be God's based on what I remember His voice sounding like . . . I believed it and then I had the responsibility in faith to move and anchor [that action] in the fact that God is good, and He would provide us evidence of that—either by answering what we were asking Him to do, which was to spare our daughter's life, or by comforting us in the loss. Either way, it's evidence of Him being good.[23]

A skeptic might say, "Of course he can say that because it all worked out for him in the end. His little girl didn't die, but mine did. How am I supposed to hope in a God who saves one life and takes another?" That's a difficult yet valid question to pose. Unfortunately, while it's understandable to feel extremely unsatisfied when asked to continue trusting in the goodness of God after a tragic event, the hope offered by any other perspective is even more disappointing. However, pointing out the limitations of non-biblical worldviews provides little comfort to someone who has experienced life-altering trauma. We need a better response.

Thankfully, the Bible does have an answer, and Spencer Te'o managed to capture it simply and beautifully. Notice that Spence's hope was grounded—anchored, as he put it—in the goodness of God, not the end result of his situation, or his ability to bring his desired outcome to fruition. He wasn't sure God had promised that his daughter would survive, but he was convinced that God is good. That conviction did not come after his daughter survived her surgery—he was fully convinced of it before she was born, before the ultrasound revealed that there were any problems at all. Because he believed in the goodness of God, he was able to recognize that either outcome would reflect that goodness, rather than defining God's goodness based on the outcome.

Would Spence have mourned for his daughter if she had died? Of course! That would have been a devastatingly painful event. However, his hope in God's goodness would have given him assurance of the resurrection and the promise that he would be reunited with her one day—not just for a few decades, but for all eternity—a promise shared by all who place their hope and faith in Jesus (1 Thessalonians 4:13-18).

The point of Spence's testimony is that neither the healing nor the loss of his daughter would have altered the truth that God is good, nor his conviction of that reality. That is what hope looks like, and that is how biblical hope works.

The Te'os are neither the first nor will they be the last to face the challenge of having a severely ill child, and not all have the happy ending this one appears to have. I say "appears to" because living with kidney disease or kidney failure is no picnic. It requires constant vigilance and consistent treatment, both of which will ultimately fail unless a transplant donor is found, which itself is a long, complex, and complicated process due to the demand greatly exceeding the supply. It also means someone else has to volunteer one of theirs or die, and even with a high-quality match, there is always the risk of infection or rejection of the new organ. The Te'os will need to continue to hope in the goodness of God because they aren't completely out of the woods yet. In fact, truth be told, they never will be.

In fact, to be honest, neither are any of us. You might not have an infant daughter with kidney failure, but I'd wager that you or someone close to you is dealing with something equally frightening. It's not that Spencer Te'o is a spiritual superhero that he has such perspective—it's because he was convinced before that 20-week ultrasound that his God is good, and he kept believing that even when he had no assurance that his daughter's next breath wouldn't be her last.

Whether the situation you are facing is a minor annoyance like a flat tire or life-changing like having a critically ill child, real hope endures because it is not based on the severity of the challenge; it is based on the unchanging goodness of God. It has nothing to do with what I want, or wish were true, or any reality I can fashion through hard work, determination, careful planning, or a positive attitude. It is founded purely on the character of God Himself.

Chapter Three
Understanding Waiting

The day that changed everything

In December 2015, while my wife, Crystal, and I were on what was supposed to be a romantic getaway trip between Christmas and New Year's to relax after the hustle and bustle of the holiday season, she revealed that she had been diagnosed with breast cancer. Earlier that month, she had noticed a lump in her right breast, and a mammogram had confirmed her suspicions, with the results coming just on Christmas Eve. Not wanting to spoil the holiday spirit, she had kept this secret to herself for several days. Understandably, her pent-up emotions overflowed as she shared the news with me.

I was stunned. I had no clue how to respond to this information or what to do about it. I had questions that she could not answer. Quite frankly, no one could answer most of them at the time, a fact that frustrated and scared both of us. I struggled to provide her the comfort she desperately needed in that moment. I didn't know what to think, what to do, or how to feel, which only added awkwardness to an already difficult conversation. To make matters worse, the day itself was dark and dreary, and the physical clouds did nothing but intensify the shadows of the emotional ones that hung over our heads, as you might expect.

The surrealness of the moment was shattered when, as we talked, a nurse called to schedule a more thorough, higher-resolution mammogram, jolting me back into reality. We both wanted to get this done as quickly as possible, but the proximity to the end of the year and the limited availability of doctors and hospital staff made that difficult. The earliest available time was on December 30th, which presented some inconveniences, but clearly, priorities needed to be adjusted, so we took it.

About an hour after the scheduling nurse called, we received another call from someone in the billing office to review the financial arrangements. I was suddenly faced with how little I understood about our insurance coverage and how it worked. When the billing lady informed me that our responsibility for this one exam would exceed $2000, I balked in disbelief. Until that moment, my experience had been limited to $25 copays for routine office visits and searching for receipts for over-the-counter items that would qualify for reimbursement from our flexible spending account, so I wasn't ready for such a large amount.

She explained that part of that amount was our annual deductible, which we hadn't used at all that year, and the rest was our share of coinsurance that would count toward our out-of-pocket maximum. I heard the words, but honestly, I didn't truly understand what she was saying. However, this was my wife we were discussing, and this was cancer, so I was determined to do what had to be done—we could figure out the finances later.

Recognizing my ignorance and knowing much better than I did what the road ahead of us looked like, the billing lady gently suggested that we postpone the test until after the first of the year. Our insurance deductible would reset in a few days, and any money we spent in the current calendar year would essentially be wasted. We would still end up paying the same amount for this particular test in 2016, but it would at least count towards that year's out-of-pocket expenses, saving us money in the long run.

Initially, I was determined to keep the appointment on December 30, but as we discussed options, I recognized the wisdom of her advice and ultimately agreed to reschedule. As I hung up, a sick feeling settled in the pit of my stomach. I was appalled that I had just made a decision about my wife's care based on money. What kind of husband does that?

There I was, less than two hours into this new and frightening phase of life, already struggling to give her the emotional support she needed, and the first practical thing I did was make a cold, calculated business decision. I felt like a heel. My instincts said the right thing to do was to act quickly in the face of a life-threatening situation, but when the very first opportunity to take action arose, what did I do? I waited. And why did I wait? Money. In that moment, as reasonable and justifiable as my choice was, I couldn't have felt more disgusted with myself.

Cancer means waiting

Thus began a new chapter in my life that would bring many unexpected experiences, one of which was learning the discipline of waiting. It started with that first advanced mammogram. Even today, I remember impatiently waiting for the day of the test, hoping that my anxiety would somehow justify the decision to postpone and cleanse my palate of the dreadful taste it left behind. I clearly recall arriving with Crystal at the hospital before dawn, writing my check, and then sitting down to wait, first for her to be called back, and then for her to return. It felt anti-climactic when we left that day knowing no more than when we arrived, except that we now had to wait for the results and discuss what they meant with a doctor.

In the days that followed, I quickly learned that when you get cancer, you don't just get one new doctor; you gain dozens of them. This is because cancer and its treatment impact every system in the body, no matter where it manifests—quite literally from the top of your head to the bottom of your feet. Hair, skin, brain, eyes, bones, teeth, nerves, heart, lungs, blood vessels, lymph nodes, stomach, pancreas, gallbladder, intestines, kidneys, liver, thyroid, reproductive organs, hands, joints, feet—you name it; my wife has a doctor for it due to breast cancer. Each of them is a specialist, and you must see them all.

Having more doctors means more appointments; more appointments lead to increased waiting for those appointment days to arrive and more waiting on the appointment days themselves for the doctor who is inevitably running behind schedule. Additionally, more doctors mean more tests and procedures, each needing to be scheduled and having its own waitlist, even for something as simple as a blood draw. Each test also requires a waiting period while it's analyzed, read, or interpreted, and then discussed with a doctor, resulting in—you guessed it—more appointments and more waiting.

That's just the routine stuff. There are bigger things, like surgeries, radiation treatments, and chemotherapy infusions, each of which is a complex event that requires preparation, execution, and follow-up steps occurring in a specific order. Furthermore, each must be coordinated and spaced out to ensure that the patient does not experience excessive risk or trauma at any given time. Waiting is intentionally built into the process.

Understanding Waiting

There are also home-based therapies that, to be done correctly, require a commitment to dedicate the necessary time. For example, in my wife's case, the cancer had spread to some lymph nodes in her right armpit, a common occurrence for breast cancer patients, so they were removed during her right mastectomy. This led to a condition called lymphedema, where lymphatic fluid begins to accumulate in the arm tissue because there are not enough lymph nodes to act as pumps that keep the fluid moving throughout the body. If left untreated, this fluid can cause swelling that may eventually obstruct the blood supply to the limb, leading to tissue necrosis that could necessitate amputation.

To combat this, in addition to always wearing a compression sleeve on her arm, she had to spend an hour and a half every day in an apparatus we affectionately referred to as her "machine." This therapy involved putting on a garment that looked like a Michelin Man suit and was connected by hoses to an air pump. The pump would sequentially inflate and deflate a series of air chambers in the suit to force the fluid up her arm, down her torso, and into her leg.

During each session she had to remain prone, encased in this thing, with her right arm elevated to facilitate fluid draining, leaving not much to do but wait for the cycle to finish. Typically, someone else (usually me) had to be close by to assist, because she needed help putting it on and getting things connected and was effectively immobilized until it was over. She did this treatment religiously every day for well over a year until the doctor determined the compression garment was sufficient to control the lymphedema. That's over 550 hours of waiting because of one simple process.

Then there are emergency situations that lead to unscheduled visits to the hospital. These can be triggered by drug reactions, falls due to chemo-induced neuropathy in the feet, or an inability to fend off common infections because of a weakened immune system. Each of these scenarios entails a wait in the emergency room, followed by a wait in an emergency department (ED) treatment room, often followed by a wait to be admitted to an ED observation room or a hospital bed, and finally, a wait to be stable enough to be discharged and sent home. Hours quickly turn into days, and sometimes weeks, of waiting, waiting, and more waiting.

No one likes to wait

Although living with a chronic disease such as cancer seems to accentuate it, waiting is an experience we are all familiar with and, I would wager, none of us find particularly appealing. Much study and creative effort has been spent on the topic of waiting in an attempt to reduce its impact on our lives by not only figuring out how to make things go faster but also by managing our perception of the passage of time.

One particularly ingenious strategy was adopted by the Heinz company in the mid-1970s through a TV and print advertising campaign to market their ketchup. At that time, ketchup came in glass bottles instead of squeezable plastic containers and was notorious for being difficult to pour. This was especially true for the Heinz brand, which took pride in the thick consistency of its ketchup compared to the thinner products from its competitors. Countless debates occurred in restaurants and at picnic tables among self-proclaimed experts about the proper technique for getting the ketchup to flow.

Instead of denying their customers' frustrations with pouring ketchup, Heinz chose to embrace them. With Carly Simon singing the chorus of her pop hit *"Anticipation"* in the background, the TV ads showcased various vignettes of people waiting for the ketchup to flow while a narrator remarked on how thick and rich the ketchup was, making the wait worthwhile. Their print ads in magazines displayed a full white page featuring an opened upside-down ketchup bottle (with no ketchup pouring out, naturally) alongside the simple slogan, "It's slow good."

Generally speaking, though, most of us don't view waiting as a positive experience. We check traffic reports each morning to find the quickest route to work. Many people try to stuff as much as possible into carry-on luggage and then cram as many bags as they can into the overhead bins on airplanes, even if they don't need to pay extra to check them, simply to avoid waiting to retrieve them from the baggage carousel at their destination. Most children, along with several adults I know, start the countdown to next year's Christmas right after this year's ends, all the while acting as if they were in timeout.

We choose checkout lines based on how quickly we think the people already in line will move and become perturbed when someone who would have been behind us enters a different line and leaves first. When you stop and think about it, you begin to realize that we put an insane amount of energy and effort into trying to avoid or reduce wait times, even if those strategies do not affect at all when the event we're waiting for will happen.

David H. Maister, a former professor at Harvard School of Business, six-time best-selling author, and world-renowned authority on the management of professional service firms, wrote an article in 2005 on *The Psychology of Waiting Lines*[24] in which he proposes his First and Second Laws of Service. The first essentially says that a satisfied customer is one who rates his experience after a given service interaction as better than his expectation going into it. The more his experience exceeds his expectations, the more satisfied he is; the more his experience falls short of his expectations, the more dissatisfied he is.

The second says that the earlier an influence on the customer's perception is introduced into the interaction, the greater its impact, be it positive or negative. Since waiting is one of the most significant elements of a customer's perception of a service interaction, the bulk of Maister's article is spent discussing the following eight factors that make wait times seem longer and how service providers can use this insight to improve a customer's perception of their wait time:

1. Unoccupied time feels longer than occupied time.
2. People want to get started.
3. Anxiety makes waits seem longer.
4. Uncertain waits are longer than known, finite waits.
5. Unexplained waits are longer than explained waits.
6. Unfair waits are longer than equitable waits.
7. The more valuable the service, the longer the customer will wait.
8. Solo waits feel longer than group waits.

From this, it would appear that the Heinz ad executives were about 30 years ahead of their time. Whether they realized it or not, they successfully leveraged Maister's seventh point by stressing that the taste and texture of their ketchup were so good that it didn't matter how long it took for the product to pour. They were so successful, in fact, that I not only remember the ads 50 years later, but I still relish the memory of waiting for that ketchup to come out of the bottle.

All of Maister's strategies are based on the fundamental assumption that no one likes to wait. He argued that the actual amount of time spent waiting is not nearly as important as how a customer perceives his waiting experience. Therefore, his strategies for improving customer satisfaction were more focused on addressing the customer's expectations about waiting for service than the quality of the service rendered.

Even though I understand from my own experiences with customer service wait times that Dr. Maister's ideas made a lot of sense, I felt somewhat skeptical about applying his theories to help me understand hope and waiting in the Scriptures. For one, biblical hope, which is a deep confidence in the goodness of God, feels too substantial to be simply a psychological tactic to ease my feelings about waiting. Additionally, I don't know of a single example in the Bible where God asked anyone to submit a customer satisfaction survey. While my flat tire experience changed my perspective on what "good" means, it wasn't meant to adjust my rating of His performance from 4 to 5 out of 5 stars. There had to be more to hope than just making me feel better about waiting. I needed to explore it more deeply.

No hope without waiting

The Apostle Paul was a big proponent of hope, so I believed his writings would be a suitable place to begin. Hope was not only a fundamental aspect of his theology, but it was also a vital part of his everyday speech. The word "hope" appears at least once in each of his epistles, except for 2 Timothy, where he still clearly conveys his hope even though he does not explicitly use the term (2 Timothy 4:6-8). Luke cites him making references to hope seven times in the last six chapters of Acts during his various trial defenses, consistently asserting that his hope in the resurrection was the reason he was put on trial by the Jews and ultimately compelled to appeal to Caesar.

Paul's most concentrated use of the word "hope" is found in the book of Romans. After explaining that we, like Abraham, are justified by faith in Christ in chapters 4 and 5, he discusses the struggle we still face with the presence of sin in our daily lives in chapters 6 and 7. He carries this discussion into chapter 8, reaffirming that because we have the Spirit of God within us, we can choose to set our minds on the things of the Spirit rather than the things of the flesh, anticipating the day when our bodies will be freed from the presence of sin, just as our souls have already been saved from the power of sin. Regarding the redemption of our bodies, he states:

> For in hope we have been saved, but hope that is seen is not hope; for who hopes for what he already sees? But if we hope for what we do not see, with perseverance we wait eagerly for it. (Romans 8:24-25)

Hope that is seen is not hope. This did not come as a shock or surprise to me, as it aligns perfectly with the understanding from Hebrews 11 that hope is the conviction of unseen things. However, Paul extends this idea by pushing it to what he clearly believes is its direct, logical, and practical conclusion, which you might find unexpected, as I did: if we hope for something, we wait for it.

In other words, it is impossible to have hope without waiting.

Ugh. This was not at all the connection I expected to find, but there it was in plain, simple language. Instinctively, I saw this as a devastatingly awful idea. I love hope, but I hate waiting. In fact, I despise it, and I don't need an expert like Maister to tell me so. I freely admit that I'm the guy who will take a 20-minute detour around a 10-minute traffic jam simply to preserve the illusion that I'm getting to my destination faster by continuing to move. What made it worse was that I thought hope was supposed to help me deal with my problems involving waiting. Instead, to my chagrin, I discovered that Paul says hope and waiting are a package deal: you can't have one without the other.

Once I managed to set aside my initial visceral reaction, I began to recognize that Paul's argument is both reasonable and sound. Since hope is confidence in unseen things, if I can see them, there's no longer a reason to hope for them. Even Pinocchio understands that if I have something, there's no reason to wish for it anymore because it exists now. Therefore, if I can't see it but am confident it exists, I must wait until I can see it. Once I see it, I can no longer hope for it because it is no longer unseen. Conversely, as long as I can't see it, I must hope for it; this also means I must wait for it. This isn't circular reasoning; rather, it demonstrates the universal truth that waiting is an unavoidable aspect of hope's very essence.

In fact, if you test the notion of the non-severability of hope and waiting against any of the definitions we've discussed, you will find that this principle is not limited to the biblical understanding but holds true in any worldview you choose to adopt. If you're wishing on a star for something, it's because you don't have it yet, which means you're waiting for your wish to be granted. And when the dream that you dream eventually comes true, there's no longer any reason to wish for it.

Similarly, for you to have a reasonable expectation that something good will happen when the sun rises tomorrow, it must still be today, meaning you are waiting for tomorrow to come. As soon as dawn breaks and the sun appears, what was tomorrow becomes today, and hope vanishes because it has moved to the next tomorrow, which you must now wait for once again. In that same vein, when you've made your passion happen, when your persistence and determination have paid off, or when you've achieved your goal, poof—hope disappears because it is no longer necessary, as the thing you were striving for has finally materialized. Until it does, however, you wait.

How a simple, logical, self-evident truth can be so easily overlooked defies explanation, yet it escaped my attention for longer than I care to admit. However, once I saw it in Romans, the pairing of hoping and waiting that I had seen in other places in the Bible began to make more sense and felt more natural, like these:

> And now, Lord, for what do I wait? My hope is in You. (Psalm 39:7)

> My soul, wait in silence for God only, for my hope is from Him. (Psalm 62:5)

Additionally, I noticed other instances in which the exact words are not used, but the concepts are:

> I waited patiently for the LORD; and He inclined to me and heard my cry. He brought me up out of the pit of destruction, out of the miry clay, And He set my feet upon a rock making my footsteps firm. (Psalm 40:1-2)

> I would have despaired unless I had believed that I would see the goodness of the LORD in the land of the living. Wait for the LORD; be strong and let your heart take courage; yes, wait for the LORD. (Psalm 27:13-14)

The connection between hope and waiting is even clearer in Hebrew. Of the five Hebrew words in the Old Testament translated as "hope" in English, three of them, including the most common, derive from roots that mean "to wait." The other two focus on the idea of looking forward expecting something to happen, or the idea of trusting, as in looking to someone or something for support. Both of those roots also have variants that mean "to wait."

Consequently, numerous wordplays and allusions linking waiting with hope appear when reading these verses in Hebrew that are lost in English, including the intrinsic essence of waiting within the nature of hope. However, once you recognize that the two are fundamentally connected, not only can you begin to identify them even in English, but you can also clearly see that Paul was not introducing something new in Romans 8:25; instead, he was referencing a truth that is underscored dozens of times in the Old Testament.

A change of perspective

As I began to recalibrate my perspective on hope to include the element of waiting, a couple of concepts began to crystalize. The first was understanding that the reason I find waiting so incredibly difficult is that it forces me to acknowledge my dependence on something unseen, which means it's out of my control. Although my actual track record with things that are under my control would argue otherwise, my natural inclination is to believe that if I could just get my grimy little hands on that one variable, I could produce a better result than anyone else, including God—nay, especially God. Waiting underscores the fact that I am dependent, that I am powerless to affect either the outcome of my choosing or its timing. By nature, I very much want *"Invictus"* to be true, but the inescapability of waiting proves that it very much is not.

Waiting is a struggle for control, and hope is a question of confidence. Therefore, the degree of confidence I have in whoever or whatever has control in each situation determines not only the strength of my hope but also the manner in which I wait. My instinct is to have greater confidence in my ability than anyone else's, so I yearn for control. But when I don't have it, I chafe, which makes waiting feel difficult and frustrating.

The second adjustment I had to make was to view waiting as good. If hope is absolute confidence in the goodness of God, and waiting is inherent in hope, then waiting is good. That's not to say that every form of delay is necessarily a good thing. I am not wise or presumptuous enough to suggest that being stranded due to a flight cancellation, being stuck in a checkout line behind a lady wanting to use 23 product-specific coupons, or missing a work deadline because of a coworker's incompetence is good, but I do believe that my hope in the goodness of God influences the way I view and respond to the waiting created in those situations.

I also believe that behaviors such as procrastination and indecisiveness are not waiting but irresponsibility masquerading as waiting. God does give us responsibilities and control over certain things, and delays arising from our mismanagement of those things are not the same as waiting, which occurs when we legitimately lack control.

Nevertheless, the reality is that I instinctively view waiting of any kind as bad. Particularly when I feel frustrated by it, I tend to blame God, without caring too terribly much whether He is actually responsible or not. Typically, my argument for doing so is that, since He is the all-powerful God and I have placed my hope in Him, He is therefore responsible for the wait I am experiencing, which obligates Him to resolve the situation to my liking. While those points are true—He is the all-powerful God, I have placed my hope in Him, and He is in control of my circumstances—the conclusion is wrong. It fails to consider another truth we've already established: everything He does is good because that's all He can do; otherwise, He wouldn't be God. As a result, every wait instigated by God is inherently good, regardless of my opinion on the matter.

Ironically, once a correct understanding of God's goodness is established, it becomes unnecessary to determine whether a specific waiting event is induced by Him. If I assert His control over my travel plans, I must deem any flight cancellation as good. If I hold Him responsible for placing the coupon lady ahead of me in line, I must accept her as a blessing. If I believe He is accountable for making me reliant on Dudley DoNothing, then I have to concede that the missed deadline and all the resulting consequences are the best outcome. Conversely, if someone or something else is responsible for those situations, then not only do I not have a quarrel with God, but I can trust that He is greater than any other entity and that, because of His goodness, He will supersede anything that is genuinely detrimental to His desire for my well-being.

This is precisely the point Paul makes in the remainder of Romans 8, right after establishing the connection between hope and waiting. There are several verses in Romans 8:26-39 that are often quoted but are frequently misunderstood and misapplied, as those quoting them do so outside the context of the entire argument. A classic example is verse 28: "And we know that God causes all things to work together for good to those who love God, to those who are called according to His purpose." Inevitably, we impose our own definition of good onto this verse, which seriously distorts what Paul is conveying.

When we overlay our idea of what it means for things to work out for good, we often treat this verse as a blank check, expecting God to make things turn out the way we think we want them. In context, Paul is discussing hope—hope grounded in the goodness of God, not in our perception of what is good. He is not promising, like George Harrison, that "everything's gonna be alright, little darlin'," but rather is urging us to endure through the sufferings of the present time, assured of God's promises to one day free our bodies from the presence of sin and to have the Holy Spirit intercede on our behalf while we await that day to arrive.

That said, waiting is still a hard thing to do. As we progressed through our cancer journey, I learned to pace myself, which mostly involved managing my expectations about how long certain events would take, but also included preparing for things I knew would eventually happen. For instance, we initially treated the first few ER visits as if they were exceptional circumstances, but soon realized they would be more common than we would have liked.

Gradually, we learned that we could manage those events more effectively and comfortably with some advanced preparation. We both started keeping "go" bags ready, containing everything we needed to handle situations that could arise whenever we had to leave the house, and we made adjustments to them regularly as we discovered what we had forgotten or what was unnecessary. Eventually, we specialized the "go" bags: one for brief trips, like to the store, a friend's house, or a routine doctor visit, one for ER trips, and one for planned hospital stays.

We learned which ERs to go to, and which to avoid. I learned to use medical terminology in a way that demonstrated I knew what I was talking about without seeming like I was trying to tell the professionals what to do. I learned how to talk to the staff and how to identify who was really in charge and could do something to expedite my wife's care. I learned to recognize the difference between the sound of a normal trip to the bathroom and a desperate one. I learned how to sleep upright with one ear open, and how to wake up quickly, alert and focused, at the drop of a pin.

All these things helped manage the waiting, but none of them eliminated it or changed my feelings about it. Eventually, I came to accept waiting as a part of life—it's inconvenient and unpleasant, but necessary. The most frustrating aspect was that I not only had to handle my own waiting but also the waiting of others.

You don't realize how connected you are until a cancer diagnosis hits social media. Hundreds of people pour out of the woodwork, all genuinely concerned, wanting to offer support and encouragement, and wanting to pray. The problem is that they all want information. When so many people ask about the same thing so frequently, it creates the impression that nobody can wait for an answer, and impatience tends to breed impatience.

Additionally, everyone processes news like this differently and at different rates, so I frequently had to wait for others to work through their own shock and grief to get to a point where I felt they could walk beside me in this journey instead of feeling like I needed to carry them. As a result, many of the gestures that others intended to alleviate my burden added more to it.

A devastating diagnosis

About four years and a half dozen surgeries after the original diagnosis, things were looking quite good. Crystal's routine scans showed no additional signs of cancer, and she had finally been able to have her right breast reconstructed. Besides the cosmetic and emotional benefits, reconstruction also offered several practical advantages, the most notable being the transplantation of lymph nodes that her body wasn't using from her groin to replace those that had been removed from under her arm. The surgeon informed us that, while he was hopeful the transplanted nodes would alleviate her lymphedema, most of his patients still had to wear a sleeve for at least part of the time. In Crystal's case, however, those little pumps activated immediately and began draining fluid from her arm. After several follow-up visits with progressively improving numbers, the surgeon told us that if her numbers remained steady for one more month, she would no longer need to wear a sleeve at all.

We were ecstatic. In a sense, once you're a cancer patient, you're always a cancer patient because of the constant screenings, but the prospect of being able to ditch the sleeve symbolized finally closing this chapter in our lives and moving on. I started planning a trip to France to celebrate, as it had always been her dream to see the Eiffel Tower and visit Monet's Garden.

The very next week, the world was shut down because of COVID-19, and we received the results of her latest set of scans. It wasn't over. The cancer had returned. When breast cancer metastasizes, it typically appears in the brain, bones, liver, or lungs. Fortunately, her organs were all clear, but her bones were not. There were small tumors on her ribs and one of her hip bones, but the largest and most concerning ones were located on her spine, in the lower thoracic and upper lumbar regions. For multiple reasons now, France would have to wait—and there's that blasted word again.

At first it appeared that this would only involve extending our trusty tried-and-true routines. However, I soon had to quickly come to grips with the fact that this situation was different from before. A metastatic diagnosis automatically designates stage 4—and there is no stage 5. Bone cancer, in any form, is incredibly painful. There was no discussion about surgically removing the tumors, because you can't do that kind of thing with bones the way you can with soft tissue. The approach to tackle this new problem was chemotherapy. Thankfully, it was an oral medication that she could take at home. Unfortunately, it was a toxic chemical accompanied by some nasty side effects. Extreme care needed to be exercised when handling the drug, as it could absorb through the skin. Its purpose was to eliminate estrogen, the hormone her type of cancer thrives on, and it was potent enough to cause severe harm to healthy individuals, both male and female, necessitating utmost caution during handling. Crystal had to wear gloves whenever she touched the pills, even when placing them in her mouth, and then immediately dispose of the gloves to prevent leaving traces of the drug behind.

Nevertheless, we adapted to the challenges. Ironically, while COVID restrictions made accessing medical care a bit more difficult, the precautions everyone was taking generally worked in our favor, providing additional protection for her weakened immune system. The drug worked for about a year, keeping the cancer's growth in check, but then it stopped—something I later learned was expected as the disease became less responsive to the effects of the treatment. At that point, our trusted oncologist, who had been a strong ally and advocate since the initial diagnosis, told us that she needed to refer us to another doctor who specializes in trial drugs because there was nothing more she could do for us.

I was devastated. What did she mean, that there was nothing more she could do? Was there really nothing more anyone could do? Why did she have to hand us off to someone else? Throughout the entire journey, Crystal had bucked all the normal trends. If the studies indicated that 98% of patients would respond to a drug a certain way, she would respond differently. If less than 2% experienced a particular side effect, she was guaranteed to experience it in full force. Even her response to the lymph node transplant proved she was a one-percenter. It had taken years for our doctor to learn to accept that Crystal was going to defy the numbers and how to treat her accordingly. Now she was going to ditch us? I felt betrayed, as if the whole floor, not just the rug, had been ripped out from beneath me.

A trial oncologist meant drug trials. Not only did that mean that the drugs aren't fully proven to work and that data on side effects and how to manage them is limited, but it also meant that you aren't guaranteed to be in the group receiving the treatment. You could end up in the control group receiving a placebo. Being willing to take the risk of not treating your illness for the sake of advancing science reveals a lot about where you are in the cancer journey, and I didn't like what it would say about me if I agreed to Crystal entering a trial.

To my surprise, the trial oncologist did not immediately recommend a trial medication. Instead, she prescribed an FDA-approved drug and told us that when, not if, this one stopped working, the only remaining options would be trials. This medication would not cure or kill the existing disease, but it would keep it at bay and should help prevent new tumors from developing. She cautioned us not to get ahead of ourselves, yet the reality was that eventually this drug would stop being effective, and when that day came, the options would be more limited, have a more severe impact on the body, and likely be less effective. When we asked how long we might expect the drug to be effective, she said the longest one of her patients had been on the drug was three years, but the average was nine months.

Feeling the weight

That was the day I perceptibly felt the weight of the burden for the first time. There was no longer any concept of a cure on this journey. Death was no longer just a possibility or an eventuality; it was an imminent reality. The goal was no longer to solve a problem but to delay the inevitable for as long as possible. Waiting was no longer an annoying consequence or incidental encumbrance in the pursuit of some other objective. Instead, suddenly, waiting itself became the objective, and the fact that we were starting to attach numbers to it added to its gravity.

In spite of this unexpected turn of events, I did not lose hope. I never questioned God's goodness, nor did it ever cross my mind to do so. I didn't feel lost, abandoned, or desperate. I did not fear death, neither for her nor for myself. I knew we were both spiritually prepared for death, and I felt I was emotionally and intellectually ready (at least as much as anyone can be) for the experience of death. What I was unprepared for was the heaviness of waiting for death, especially in light of our declared strategy to extend the waiting as long as we could.

For the first time in five and a half years, I began to feel my knees buckle, much like those of Olympian weightlifters attempting to hold 500 pounds of iron over their heads. Unlike an Olympian, however, I could not drop my bar after a few seconds. I had to hold mine for days, weeks, months, or, ironically, hopefully longer. The indefinite timing of an inevitable result seemed to add its own weight to the burden, a phenomenon I described to my friend Greg as the weight of the wait.

I felt it most in my worship. I became unable to sing, not because there was no joy or hope in my heart, but because every time I tried, I cried like a baby. Even the most encouraging, upbeat praise songs would trigger an emotional response. I stopped trying to sing out loud, opting to recite the words in my head and heart, but even that brought me to tears. It reached a point where my goal in church was no longer to serve or be ministered to, but to see if I could keep my composure for 75 minutes. For months, I inexplicably failed to do even that, praying every Sunday that the deacons had remembered to restock the tissue boxes and that no one would notice what a complete blubbering fool I had become.

Oh, and I prayed a lot, but, surprisingly, not for healing from cancer. What I prayed for was relief from the weight. I never used those words, but in hindsight, I realize that's what I was doing. What I prayed for was to understand how to endure this ordeal. I knew others were watching, and I felt a responsibility to represent God well during this time, but weeping through worship services seemed to send a completely different message. Unfortunately, even prayer became a problem. In private, one-on-one, I had no trouble talking to Him, but praying out loud in public was impossible without breaking down in tears. Even giving thanks for a meal was enough to make me tear up, no matter how brief and simple the prayer was. Why? To this day, I honestly have no idea. All I know is that it was both embarrassing and confusing.

A friend leads the way

Around the same time we were referred to the trial oncologist, a college friend of mine and his wife contracted COVID. They both had a tough time with it. She recovered, but he did not. Eventually, he was admitted to a university hospital several hours away from their home and the church he pastored because the local hospital could not handle a case as severe as his. As I read his wife's nearly daily posts on Caringbridge.com, it quickly became clear to me that he would likely never leave the hospital alive.

However, it was neither curiosity nor concern for his condition that made me eagerly await her next journal entry, but rather the way she wrote them. She wrote candidly, transparently, and with raw honesty about her daily struggles: the good, the bad, the ups, and the downs. She shared the things that gave her hope, as well as the days when it seemed she had none. Every post radiated her unwavering faith in God. She understood, better than the rest of us, where this story was heading, and the weight of her wait was evident. What fascinated me was how that weight never crushed her hope. There were days when her back bent and her knees scraped the ground under the burden, yet it never broke her faith. She didn't just deal with the weight—she dealt with it well and did so for over three months until the day they turned off the machines keeping him alive.

I was enthralled with the whole experience. Not because I was amazed by her faith and fortitude, which were definitely obvious and commendable, nor because we had a close relationship—which, quite frankly, we didn't—but because I recognized she was showing me the right path. My crisis was imminent, but hers was immediate; while I had time to prepare, she was given no such advantage. There was much I could relate to.

I could visualize the hospital scenes she described. I could hear the voices of the hospital staff as she got to know them and relayed conversations she had with them. I was all too familiar with the awkward discomfort of having a meal or occupying a bed alone. She cried. She was scared. But she had hope, and she shared it in ways that at that time I hadn't and couldn't. She was open about her struggles, sharing both the good and the bad. She sought to encourage the families of other patients and the hospital staff she befriended. She leaned heavily on God's word. Even when it became clear that her husband would not recover, her tone didn't change. She would be the first to tell you she's no spiritual giant, yet she was not crushed under a weight whose mere shadow had debilitated me.

I needed to pay attention and take notes. My turn was coming, and I clearly wasn't ready. I was receiving a gift: an example of what it looks like to walk that road well, with faith and hope, along with the time to prepare for it. If I was going to carry my weight well, I needed to learn from her example.

I wish I could tell you that a light went on immediately, that I identified the point God wanted me to learn as I observed my friend's widow process her grief, and that it produced a radical change in me right away. It didn't happen that way. I had seen hope and faith in action, and I had begun to recognize my struggle with waiting, but I didn't understand why God kept urging me to pay attention to that situation. The best I could figure was that He was preparing me for my wife to die.

But that didn't happen. At first, our objectives were very short-term. Make it to Christmas. Get through the birth of our second grandson in January. Make it to Easter. Easter was the furthest we dared to hope for, and we were at peace with that. In fact, my wife told the Lord that if He allowed her to live until Easter, she'd be ready to go any time after that. He didn't seem to object, and neither did I. After all, He had given me an example to follow.

The new combination of disease and drug didn't take long to begin taking its toll. Bone cancer is extremely painful, so narcotics quickly became part of the maintenance drug regimen. New, harsher side effects emerged. Sleep became harder to come by, and less restful when it occurred. Mobility assistive devices became necessary first outside the home and then inside as well, because the neuropathy in her feet became so intense that she was constantly at risk of falling, which happened several times. Each day, it seemed we were inching closer to the inevitable and now expected conclusion; yet the scans kept showing that the disease was not progressing. "Stable" was the term the radiologists used.

The first Easter came and went, as did the second and the third. Collateral damage increased, but slowly. The disease remained stable. I regained my ability to sing. I would still tear up when I prayed out loud, but if I kept it short, it didn't typically get out of control, and everyone else appreciated my brevity.

Unlike my friend's widow, who endured a painful, three-month journey, the inescapable inevitability we anticipated never seemed to arrive. Crystal took that initial drug for three and a half years before it lost effectiveness—the longest the oncologist had ever treated a patient with that drug. After that, she began two other chemotherapy regimens but had to stop due to intolerable side effects, and as I write this, she is currently on a third.

Remarkably, none of them are trial therapies, but they are treatments that were not available when we first met with the trial oncologist. Thanks to the generosity of others, I was able to take her to Paris, and we enjoyed a spectacularly beautiful day in Monet's Garden. There was a time when waiting four months to see the birth of the second grandchild felt like a stretch goal; now, it's hard to believe the third one is already a year old.

All this begs the question of what He really wanted me to learn from my friend's bout with COVID if it wasn't to prepare me for my wife's death, which is still a future event. Why did He let me get so anxious over something that wouldn't happen for years? Why make me aware of my struggles with waiting and then make me wait even longer? If I weren't so convinced that God is good, I would have thought He was just rubbing my nose in it. Even so, it still left me confused. There had to be more that I hadn't yet understood.

Chapter Four
Why God Makes Us Wait

What was He thinking?

In an effort to figure out what else I was missing, I reviewed what I had discovered so far.

- Hope is conviction in an unseen reality, namely, God.
- God is good because that is the only thing He can be, and He does good because that is the only thing He can do; otherwise, He would not be God.
- It is impossible to have hope without waiting.
- Because hope is confidence in the goodness of God, and waiting is a component of hope, waiting is good.

Chances are you're still wrestling with that last one. I certainly was when I wrote that list down on paper for the first time. There are days when I'm not as convinced as I should be because, even when I know in my head and heart that waiting is good, it usually doesn't feel good.

Why is that? We really want to believe that God is good, but let's face it—when you're stuck in a seemingly endless wait queue, for something you desperately need or want, it's really hard to envision Him as anything but bad.

We picture Him acting like a mischievous 12-year-old boy focusing the rays of the sun with a big cosmic magnifying glass on our little ant tails, gleefully watching us scramble in pain and confusion while simultaneously asking us to be grateful for the experience. This kind of image contradicts the Bible's explicit statements that God is good, yet sadly, it is precisely how many—or dare I say most—perceive God. Ironically, in their minds, the very concept of hope, regardless of how it is defined or understood, seems to prove that God (if He exists at all) is nothing more than a cosmic killjoy, amusing Himself by playing keep-away with things that matter to us.

Even if you disagree with the characterization of God as a bully, you still need to ask why He would allow Himself to be seen in that light. If He is powerful enough to create a world where waiting is a reality, He is also smart enough to have anticipated that we would misunderstand it. So why do it in the first place? Or, did He intend for our experience with waiting to be something different, and we distorted it through sin, just as we have with so many other things?

Regardless of how it may feel on any given day, I knew that waiting is not part of the curse, nor was it introduced into the world by sin. Granted, sin and our rebellion against God add a lot of baggage that complicates matters significantly, but there's nothing in Genesis 3:14-24 that says or implies that waiting entered human existence as a negative consequence of the fall. The idea of waiting being good drew me back to the account of creation in Genesis 1 to see if there was any evidence of waiting before the fall.

Let there be waiting

After Moses establishes the existence of God and His creation of a formless universe, he pens some of the most familiar words in the entire Bible:

> Then God said, "Let there be light"; and there was light. God saw that the light was good; and God separated the light from the darkness. God called the light day, and the darkness He called night. And there was evening and there was morning, one day. (Genesis 1:3-5)

At first blush, this seems fairly simple and straightforward: God created light. He spoke light into existence and then separated light from darkness, calling the light "day" and the darkness "night." However, a closer examination reveals some things that aren't so straightforward. The question that has captured the attention of rabbis and theologians, likely since the day after Moses wrote this down, is the source of the light, given that the sun wasn't created until the fourth day.

Some believe it was God Himself—either a manifestation of the glory of the pre-incarnate Christ or of God's shekinah glory, similar to that which filled the Holy of Holies in the tabernacle and temple. Some view this as a veiled reference to the creation of angelic beings, often referred to as luminaries. Others think that God created the essence of light in Genesis 1:3 without establishing a specific source to emanate it. Some believe there was an unidentified temporary light source that was either replaced by the sun on day four or repurposed to become the sun on that day. All we know for certain is that we have absolutely no idea what the source of the light was, aside from God's creative act, and that God found it unnecessary to clarify that question for us.

If God did not intend to explain to us how light could exist before the sun did, why did He tell us about the creation of light in the first place? To answer that question, we need to stop speculating about what He didn't tell us and focus instead on what He did.

First, we see that He spoke light into existence. This point is highlighted in several other places in Scripture, as part of establishing the deity of Jesus as the Word of God and, therefore, the creator. Second, God saw that the light was good. This is the first time God's work is described as good, and as we've already seen, it initiates a pattern repeated throughout the creation story, designed to affirm the goodness of both God's character and actions.

As we have already discussed, goodness is such an essential quality of God that He would not be God if He were not good. Therefore, it is fitting and meaningful for that truth to be established, quite literally, from day one. Third, we are told that God separated light from darkness and named them day and night, respectively. This common theme recurs throughout Scripture and sets up the dichotomy between good and evil. Jesus Himself referenced this when He explained to Nicodemus that "men loved the darkness rather than the light because their deeds were evil" (John 3:19).

Now consider the significance of the concepts introduced on the first day of creation: the deity of Christ, the goodness of God, and the diametric opposition of good and evil. It's ludicrous for me to speculate on what ideas I might have established on day one if it had been up to me, but as far as foundational principles of the universe are concerned, those are some exceptionally robust selections.

Do you know what else God established on day one along with these foundational doctrines of the faith? Waiting.

Before you accuse me of just making stuff up, take a closer look at the text. Genesis 1:5 states, "And there was evening and there was created everything at once with a single utterance, yet He chose to do it incrementally and in sequence, deferring until the very end the creation of those He loved so much that He would sacrifice His own life to redeem them. It was essential to His design to create the rhythms we now recognize as vital to life, such as activity and rest, weeks and months, and seasons and years.

How those seasons manifested themselves prior to man's fall is one of those mysteries we'll have to wait to understand until we see Him face to face, although we may have some clues based on the descriptions of the new heaven and the new earth in the Book of Revelation. Even though the introduction of sin certainly impacted the way we experience time and waiting today, the core mechanism remains intact.

It's all about pleasing God

Because time begets waiting, it also begets hope. What a marvelous idea it is that at the very heart of God's intent, design, and architecture of the universe was His desire for us to hope and to have hope! He wanted me to experience the sensation of mouth-watering anticipation as the ketchup slowly forms a glob large enough to drop onto my hamburger. He wanted us to know the joy and excitement brought about by the expectations of monumental events in our lives, like a wedding day or the birth of a child. Even the spine-tingling sensation we feel from the roar of a stadium full of fans at the beginning of a championship game or a concert was part of His design for how He wanted us to experience life.

Why is time such an important component of God's plans for the world and for us? Why did He choose to establish this particular mechanism, including the corollary concepts of waiting and hope, as a fundamental operating principle of the universe? Fortunately, just as He explained why He placed the sun in the sky, He has also revealed why He included waiting in our lives.

Let's return to Hebrews 11 and revisit the definition of hope. Hope, as we have seen, is defined in relation to faith:

> Now faith is the assurance of things hoped for, the conviction of things not seen. (Hebrews 11:1)

Again, we've already discussed the difference between faith and hope and the fact that hope is a component of faith. Faith is an action based on hope.

> For by it the men of old gained approval. (Hebrews 11:2)

Here, the author sets up the rest of the chapter, where he will give examples of people who demonstrated their faith and thereby "gained approval." The Greek word used here means "to obtain a good testimony or reputation." The New International Version (NIV) translates the entire sentence as "This is what the ancients were commended for," while the English Standard Version (ESV) states, "For by it the people of old received their commendation." In other words, this is how we know that the good guys in the Bible are the good guys: because they exercised faith. To reinforce his point, the author explicitly uses the same word when discussing the first two men in his list and applies it to everyone else in verse 39. However, before delving into that conversation, he references something that has nothing to do with any human being.

> By faith we understand that the worlds were prepared by the word of God, so that what is seen was not made out of things which are visible. (Hebrews 11:3)

morning, one day." This is not merely an arbitrary label that God assigned for identification purposes. Nor was it mentioned simply to instigate debates over how long it was. If we set aside all the things we don't know (and, frankly, things we cannot know) and focus on what He does tell us, we see that on day one God created day one. On day one, God created time.

Time is an intriguing concept that has fascinated mankind since the beginning. It has been the subject of study and musings of philosophers, scientists, mathematicians, linguists, artists, historians, and theologians, as it is fundamental to the universe and everything within it.

Humans are incapable of functioning outside of time. We cannot even express ourselves without it. Every verb in every language on Earth has tense—the element of time—built into it in one way or another. We cannot objectively speed it up or slow it down. We cannot escape its effects. Though we talk about saving it, we cannot collect or store it. While some of us experience more of it than others during the span of our lives, on any given day, no one has any more than anyone else, nor can a person acquire or lose more than anyone else. We all consume it at the same rate; in fact, it is the very thing by which we define and measure rate.

Time gives order and structure to our world. It helps us govern our interactions with one another and is implied in any kind of sequencing. It controls how we earn money and, in many cases, how we spend it. We use it to describe and control the extent to which our leaders have power. We use it to label, track, and celebrate people and events that are important to us. We even use it as a measuring stick to quantify how important those things are to us.

The intentionality of God in making time a core element of His design for the universe becomes more prominent as we read the rest of the creation account. It starts with the notion that a day is comprised of an evening and a morning, a period of darkness followed by a period of light. This cycle is repeated and counted with each progressive creative step until the seventh one, when God stops creating and rests, signaling the end of that progression and creating the concept of a week.

On the fourth day, the importance of time in God's mind explodes off the page. For the first time, He gives us insight into His actions. Up to this point, God simply tells us what He did and how He intended for things to work, but in Genesis 1:14-19, He reveals His intentions, explaining the purpose behind creating the astral bodies: to separate day from night, to illuminate the earth, to govern the cycles of day and night, and to establish signs, seasons, days, and years. He didn't create the sun, moon, and stars just for us to gawk at; they were created to affirm the order and sequence of time, giving us a way to track and measure it.

The emphasis He places on order and sequencing in this passage is significant. In these five verses, besides explicitly calling out seasons, days, and years, He uses the phrases "to give light" twice, "to separate" twice, and "to govern" three times. Such repetition, particularly regarding God's intentions, does not appear anywhere else in Genesis 1. God purposefully created time, and He wanted there to be absolutely no equivocation on that point.

Finiteness and faith

But why make such a fuss over time? What makes time so important that He felt it necessary to call it out in this fashion? And what was His purpose in establishing time as one of the foundational principles of the universe, alongside the deity of Christ, the goodness of God, and the distinction between good and evil?

There are likely several valid answers to these questions, but I will focus on just two. The first is that, by creating time and enveloping us and the rest of the universe within it, He made us finite, while He is infinite. No matter what we do, no matter how powerful or intelligent we become, we cannot break free from this box of time we're in. God, on the other hand, is not only outside the box and bigger than the box, He created the box. It is the ultimate trump card, the clinching argument in any debate, and He's not afraid to use it. In fact, when He had reached His limit with Job's friends' pontifications and erroneous explanations about the nature of good and evil, and why Job found himself sitting on an ash heap, covered in sores, with his life in ruins, God spoke up and said,

> Where were you when I laid the foundation of the earth?
> Tell Me, if you have understanding,
> Who set its measurements? Since you know.
> Or who stretched the line on it?
> On what were its bases sunk?
> Or who laid its cornerstone,
> When the morning stars sang together
> And all the sons of God shouted for joy? (Job 38:4-7)

This rebuke goes on for over 70 verses between chapters 38 and 39, including this section:

> Have you understood the expanse of the earth?
> Tell Me, if you know all this.
> Where is the way to the dwelling of light?
> And darkness, where is its place,
> That you may take it to its territory
> And that you may discern the paths to its home?

> You know, for you were born then,
> And the number of your days is great!
> Have you entered the storehouses of the snow,
> Or have you seen the storehouses of the hail,
> Which I have reserved for the time of distress,
> For the day of war and battle?
> Where is the way that the light is divided,
> Or the east wind scattered on the earth? (Job 38:18-24)

Can you hear the echoes of day four of creation in this passage? Did you catch the references to "the dwelling of light" and "the way that the light is divided"? Did you notice how time is mentioned in different ways? God used His creative power, including His ability to create time, to remind us of our place in this world. We are finite; He is not. He is God, and we are not. The fact that this was the core issue in the very first temptation (Genesis 3:4) underscores the importance of establishing it on day one.

The second reason God places such a strong emphasis on time is that He intended waiting to be an essential component of our existence. When God created time, He created waiting. As we have seen, time is about order and sequencing—a point God went out of His way to stress to us in His description of day four. With any sequence of events comes the inevitability of waiting since sequenced events cannot occur simultaneously. This means that time must pass between the beginning of the first event and the start of the second, thereby creating a period of waiting. Consequently, waiting is inescapable because time is inescapable, and the nature of time inherently requires, by definition, that we wait.

The fact that God intended for us to wait is also reflected in His decision to wait until the sixth day to create man. He could have created everything at once with a single utterance, yet He chose to do it incrementally and in sequence, deferring until the very end the creation of those He loved so much that He would sacrifice His own life to redeem them. It was essential to His design to create the rhythms we now recognize as vital to life, such as activity and rest, weeks and months, and seasons and years.

How those seasons manifested themselves prior to man's fall is one of those mysteries we'll have to wait to understand until we see Him face to face, although we may have some clues based on the descriptions of the new heaven and the new earth in the Book of Revelation. Even though the introduction of sin certainly impacted the way we experience time and waiting today, the core mechanism remains intact.

It's all about pleasing God

Because time begets waiting, it also begets hope. What a marvelous idea it is that at the very heart of God's intent, design, and architecture of the universe was His desire for us to hope and to have hope! He wanted me to experience the sensation of mouth-watering anticipation as the ketchup slowly forms a glob large enough to drop onto my hamburger. He wanted us to know the joy and excitement brought about by the expectations of monumental events in our lives, like a wedding day or the birth of a child. Even the spine-tingling sensation we feel from the roar of a stadium full of fans at the beginning of a championship game or a concert was part of His design for how He wanted us to experience life.

Why is time such an important component of God's plans for the world and for us? Why did He choose to establish this particular mechanism, including the corollary concepts of waiting and hope, as a fundamental operating principle of the universe? Fortunately, just as He explained why He placed the sun in the sky, He has also revealed why He included waiting in our lives.

Let's return to Hebrews 11 and revisit the definition of hope. Hope, as we have seen, is defined in relation to faith:

> Now faith is the assurance of things hoped for, the conviction of things not seen. (Hebrews 11:1)

Again, we've already discussed the difference between faith and hope and the fact that hope is a component of faith. Faith is an action based on hope.

> For by it the men of old gained approval. (Hebrews 11:2)

Here, the author sets up the rest of the chapter, where he will give examples of people who demonstrated their faith and thereby "gained approval." The Greek word used here means "to obtain a good testimony or reputation." The New International Version (NIV) translates the entire sentence as "This is what the ancients were commended for," while the English Standard Version (ESV) states, "For by it the people of old received their commendation." In other words, this is how we know that the good guys in the Bible are the good guys: because they exercised faith. To reinforce his point, the author explicitly uses the same word when discussing the first two men in his list and applies it to everyone else in verse 39. However, before delving into that conversation, he references something that has nothing to do with any human being.

> By faith we understand that the worlds were prepared by the word of God, so that what is seen was not made out of things which are visible. (Hebrews 11:3)

Lest you think that connecting hope and waiting to the creation story is reading things into the text that aren't there, Hebrews 11:3 explicitly makes that connection. It is a direct and specific reference to Genesis 1:3, tying faith and hope (the things which are not seen), which he just defined in verse 1, to day one of creation.

A couple of verses later, we see some interesting comments about a man named Enoch. Aside from his mention in several genealogies, all we know about Enoch comes from three passages: Genesis 5:21-24, Jude 14-15, and here in Hebrews 11:5-6. Jude states that he prophesied against those who distorted the truth before the flood and applies Enoch's prophecy to false teachers in the church. Genesis 5 tells us he was the father of Methuselah and adds this curious little tidbit:

> Enoch walked with God; and he was not, for God took him. (Genesis 5:24)

If it weren't for Hebrews, there would be considerable debate over what it means that he "was not" or that "God took him." From the rest of Genesis 5, we can infer that Enoch didn't die, since his entry is the only one in that entire genealogy that does not end with the words, "and he died," but Moses doesn't state this explicitly. Fortunately, the author of Hebrews not only confirms this interpretation but also adds some additional commentary that isn't as obvious from the record in Genesis:

> By faith Enoch was taken up so that he would not see death; AND HE WAS NOT FOUND BECAUSE GOD TOOK HIM UP; for he obtained the witness that before his being taken up he was pleasing to God. (Hebrews 11:5)

There's that key thought about gaining approval or being commended, which the author identifies as the focal point of this entire chapter in verse 2. Clearly, there must have been something special about Enoch that allowed him to not see death, something no one else in history, except the prophet Elijah, has experienced. That's impressive. With all due respect to the greatest basketball player of all time and his Nike ad campaign from the 1990s, I don't want to be like Mike—I want to be like Enoch. Whatever pleasing God means, it is obviously a big deal.

Unlike identifying the source of light on the first day of creation, God made a point of having Moses call out in Genesis that Enoch pleased Him and having the author of Hebrews to elaborate further on it. It is worth mentioning that while Enoch and Elijah are the only people known who have not experienced physical death up until now, they will not be the only ones.

Paul tells us in 1 Thessalonians 4:17 that believers who are alive when Jesus returns will be taken up, similar to what we understand happened to Enoch and Elijah. It's important to note that not dying does not prove that Enoch pleased God, nor does it imply that those who were not taken up did not please Him. In fact, the author's main point in Hebrews 11 is that all these other people, from Abel onward, did please God, even though Enoch was the only one who didn't die.

Happily, the author of Hebrews explains himself and tells us exactly how Enoch pleased God:

> And without faith it is impossible to please Him, for he who comes to God must believe that He is and that He is a rewarder of those who seek Him. (Hebrews 11:6)

Enoch pleased God by walking with Him in faith—by believing that God exists, even though he couldn't see Him, by having hope in God's goodness to keep His promises, and by living his life based on that faith. We've already seen how this verse is tied to the goodness of

God, but now we see it also connects faith to hope and waiting. Follow the bouncing ball carefully:

- Without faith it is impossible to please God.
- Hope is a component of faith (faith = hope + action).
- It is impossible to hope without waiting.
- Therefore, it is impossible to please God without waiting.
- Time defines waiting.
- Therefore, time defines the mechanism for hope, which is needed for faith, which is needed to please God.

This is why God created time—to establish faith as the basis for our relationship with Him. When He created time and enveloped the entire universe in it, He mandated that waiting be an inescapable reality for everyone and everything. Why? Because waiting requires us to have hope. Why is hope essential? Because hope is a necessary component of faith. And why did He make faith mandatory? Because faith is the only way to please Him, and that's our purpose. He wanted us to please Him; therefore, He created the universe and contained it within time, ensuring that by nature and design, this is exactly what we would do.

Waiting is good

You may be familiar with images known as stereograms. The first one I ever saw was a poster-sized image hanging on the wall of a friend's home. He claimed it was a breathtaking picture, but all I could see was a jumble of indistinct colored shapes arranged in a repeating pattern, but nothing I could recognize. My friend told me I needed to focus my eyes beyond the surface of the image, a task I struggled with for a long time. However, when I finally succeeded, a majestic three-dimensional bald eagle emerged, wings spread wide as it rested on a branch of a shrub atop a mountain. I marveled at how I could stare at something so stunning for so long without seeing it.

Understanding this dynamic about time and waiting in the creation story felt similar to viewing a stereogram. While I easily recognized the references to the deity of Christ, the goodness of God, and the dichotomy between good and evil, I completely overlooked the concept that faith, by virtue of time and waiting, was also established as a foundational principle from day one. However, just as the eagle on my friend's poster blew me away, once I saw it, my perspective on waiting was entirely transformed.

God created time and encapsulated my entire existence within it, so that I would be less than He is and would have to wait; because waiting necessitates hope, which is the foundation of faith, which is the only way to please God, and what He wanted for me since before the beginning of time. He desires that I walk with Him just like Enoch did, where He enjoys the closeness of our relationship so much that He says, "Forget about going back to your place. Why don't you just come home with Me and stay?" Wouldn't that be awesome? That means waiting is awesome, too.

Still not convinced that waiting is a good thing? Let's examine this from a more pragmatic perspective. Imagine a world where you didn't have to wait for anything. My wife would love that. She adores her grandchildren and can't wait to have more, so much so that she isn't shy about playing the cancer card to encourage our adult children to speed things up. What if she didn't have to wait for my son to find a good woman, fall in love, get married, and have triplets (because who has time for three pregnancies)? Think about how much simpler things would be if we just eliminated all that unpleasant waiting stuff. One moment she has three grandkids, and the next she's got ten.

But hold on—if we're going to have all these babies right away, as precious as they are, isn't the joy in watching them grow up? Unfortunately, in this world where there's no waiting, starting as a child and growing into an adult loses its meaning. If we take away waiting, we destroy all the moments that make life special. That means there are no first times to hold an infant in your arms, no first steps, no first words. There's no longer a first birthday, first Christmas, or first day of school. Any chance for a first crush, a first date, or a first kiss is gone. Forget about driving for the first time, landing your first job, or securing your first home. In fact, in a world without waiting, nothing about life as we know it, especially the good things, holds any significance. All the moments we cherish in life prove that waiting is good.

But let's suppose for a moment that it were possible to live in a world that functions much like it does now, except that we could pick and choose the things we want and designate them to be exempt from waiting. Imagine if we could ask God for anything, and He would grant it instantly, no waiting required. Let's be honest, that's how we would really like it to work. BAM! No more cancer. Poof! An instant brand-new job (unless, of course, you want that extra vacation time in between jobs). Maybe your aspirations are a bit loftier. Presto! Your unbelieving spouse just wakes up one day and decides to follow Jesus. Sounds pretty great, doesn't it?

The problem is that such solutions completely eradicate God from the equation, converting Him, at best, to a glorified vending machine. That may be what you want, but it's not what He wants. He wants us to depend on Him, as He wants both Himself and us to experience the joy of time-bound, finite beings engaging in a worshipful and dependent relationship with an eternal, infinite God. Without faith, that simply isn't possible. Just as eliminating time and waiting from our lives robs us of those special moments we long for and treasure as significant, memorable, and precious, removing faith from our relationship with God robs us of the love, joy, and peace we can only know in Him.

Stepping back and curling up

Why then do I abhor waiting so much? There's really no way to sugarcoat this: control. I wish there were a less confrontational answer, but there's no getting around it. As we've already discussed, waiting is a question of control, specifically, who has it. I want control because I want to be God and run the world the way I see fit, at least in my little corner of it. When I'm anxious about how the bills will get paid, it's not really about financial responsibility; it's about control and how little I feel I have. When I impatiently honk my horn at the guy in front of me who is stuck in the same traffic jam, it's not about driving habits; it's about control and the fact that he's impeding me from getting where I want to go and when I want to get there. When I consistently work my tail off, but the raise or promotion never comes, it's not a question of fairness; it's about control and the fact that I'm not getting the recognition and respect I think I deserve.

This struggle for control is demonstrated throughout Abraham's life. Although he is celebrated for his faith in Hebrews 11 and recognized by Paul as the exemplary model of faith we should follow in Romans 4 and Galatians 3, in Genesis, Abraham frequently tried to maneuver through the challenging situations he faced. In a recent sermon, a good friend of mine, pastor and Bible teacher Scot Pollok, discussed Abraham's actions, noting that the opposite of faith is not fear, as many often believe, but control. Holding his hands out, palms open and facing upwards, he stated, "If faith is open-handed, this movement of trust without answers to the questions where and how and why and when, then," turning his hands over, palms down, and clenching his fists, "the opposite would be this: clamping down. My word for that is not fear but control." He went on to say that when we are afraid and wrestling with God for control, "faith does not disappear in the presence of fear, but it does step back and curl up."[25]

No matter what the issue is, no matter what the condition that causes you to wait, how you feel about waiting is directly tied to who's in control of that situation and how content you are with that arrangement. If you are content with God being in control and trust in His goodness, you possess hope, which allows you to wait with a different attitude and take actions in faith that you might not otherwise consider. Conversely, if you are discontent with God being in control—whether because you think He's doing a lousy job of it, or you would just rather manage things on your own, you struggle. If you hold to that position long enough, you will eventually find yourself in a conversation with Him akin to the one in Job 38 and 39. Whether you like it or not, you are boxed in time, and He is the one who created the box.

Being a novice waiter

I'll be honest—I struggled for a long time with this concept of waiting being about control without even realizing I had an issue with it. When we got Crystal's initial cancer diagnosis, I had already had my flat tire experience and had restructured my philosophy of life around Psalm 119:65-72. When we told our children, who were between 15 and 23 years old at the time, I distinctly remember talking them through it from that perspective. "God is good because that's all He can be, and God does good because that's all He can do," I said. "We don't know where this is going or what it means; but whatever happens, God is still good."

It was a great start and a solid foundation. It allowed me to maintain an even keel that I think shocked and surprised many people. I never got angry with God. I never asked why her, why me, why us, or why now. I never even asked God to heal her. Hundreds of others did and still are praying for that, but I never have. Not because I don't want her to be healed or because I'm trying to be some super-spiritual hero—it just never occurred to me. In fact, it wasn't until several years later when someone made a passing comment like, "It must be hard to have prayed for healing all this time" that I realized I hadn't. When I thought about why, I realized that I was so convinced of the goodness of God that I figured He wouldn't have allowed the cancer unless He had a greater purpose for it, and that He would heal her, if He chose to, when He was good and ready.

While I appeared to have mastered the goodness of God part of the lesson, I was a novice at the waiting part. I was clueless about how to manage waiting, and I did it very poorly at the beginning, both physically and mentally. I was unaware that it was also spiritual or that it added its own mass to the burden I was carrying.

Where it first began to show was not in my attitude towards God, but in my attitude towards people. From the very beginning, both Crystal and I viewed cancer as a ministry rather than a trial, so we talked about it openly. She continued to lead our church's ministry for special needs children and sought out and connected with other women who were also dealing with breast cancer, primarily to encourage them. As the news spread, one phenomenon I observed, yet did not anticipate, was that people learning about her cancer for the first time had to go through a grieving process. Shock, denial, anger, bargaining, acceptance—I witnessed all the stages on the faces of others.

The first few times I saw this, it was understandable because we were sharing with extended family and close friends, and that type of reaction is expected. But it wasn't just close friends and extended family; it was everyone, and it became annoying. I noticed I had to make a conscious effort to avoid physically tapping my foot impatiently or gesturing with my hand as if to say, "Come on, hurry up. We passed that stage 18 months ago. Get with the program and catch up already." Of course, I never voiced anything like that; that would have been unkind. But internally, it tightened me up more than a whole army of wind-up toy soldiers.

As word of her condition continued to spread and we encountered additional challenges, Crystal gained celebrity status. People were drawn to her and her story like moths to a flame. She is legitimately one of the sweetest people you'll ever meet, and her commitment to serve and lead the Special Needs ministry in spite of pain and illness was genuinely inspirational. However, I was unprepared for the degree of visibility and notoriety she attained. Through the magic of social media, she became friends with friends of friends, discussing people I had never heard of. She didn't post often, but when she did, she'd generate hundreds of responses within an hour. I could post the same thing, and it would only receive about 20% of the reactions she got. I did not begrudge her the attention she received; after all, hers was the body battling cancer and enduring chemotherapy. However, I have to admit I was jealous, nonetheless.

Clenched fists

At the same time, I was responsible for directing a large, complex, highly visible, and expensive project at work. The service provider my company chose for the job did not meet my expectations. The skill level and work ethic of most of their engineers fell far short of what was required, and the leaders seemed unable to address the issues. They severely underestimated the time, resources, and costs of the project, to the point that even before we attempted the first big task, they were already predicting an over-budget outcome. Disagreements over responsibility for expenses incurred by both sides hung like the sword of Damocles over my head for months, even after the project was finished.

I was forced to take a more hands-on approach to leading the effort than originally planned because they didn't get along with any of my other vendors who needed to participate in the project, and they scared my stakeholders to death. Finger-pointing was rampant, but ultimately, only one person would be held accountable if this became the disaster it seemed destined to become: me.

Needless to say, I was under severe tension throughout the entire three-year project. Just like Father Abraham, whatever faith I may have expressed regarding my wife's cancer, I completely abandoned on the job. I was constantly irritable and short-tempered. I slammed doors, hung up on conference calls in anger, complained, yelled, and swore. Why? Because try as I might, I could not bend the situation to my will. Delays were constant, some caused by incompetent help, others by the irrational fears of stakeholders, some by internal politics, and still others by poor choices on my part. All of them were frustrating. Every day was a fight. As I led the team through these challenges, we made steady progress, earning me a lot of accolades. Unfortunately, while it seemed that I was doing all the right things, I did most of them the wrong way. The toll on both my body and soul continued to mount as I fought harder and harder to maintain control over things I couldn't, and progressively lost control over things I shouldn't have.

About a year and a half into the project, I started to feel some soreness in my forearms that I couldn't explain. Then I noticed that the middle finger of my right hand would lock up when I tried to extend it, and it would pop painfully if I forced it past that point. The same issue started happening to the middle finger on my left hand, and then with other fingers on my right. Eventually, one morning I woke up and realized I had been clenching my fists in my sleep. I continued to ignore the issue until one night I clenched them so tightly that the pain jolted me out of a deep sleep.

Several months of physical therapy helped me relax my trigger fingers and get rid of the soreness in my forearms, although it was more than a year before I could snap my fingers again. The doctors and I attributed my pain to the stress in my life, which seemed logical. My wife was suffering from a terminal illness, and my work life was filled with nothing but problems and difficult people. At one point, I completed a Holmes-Rahe Life Stress Inventory, which assigns point values to both positive and negative life events that happened in the previous year. A score of 150-300 points indicates a 50% chance of experiencing a major stress-induced health issue, such as a heart attack or a stroke.

When I took the assessment, I scored over 400 by only considering things I had experienced in the prior three months, rather than twelve. I didn't even include "death of a spouse" (which is worth 100 points on its own) because she hadn't actually died yet. Stupidly, I was a bit proud of my ability to endure that kind of pressure without suffering more than a couple of sore arms. However, what was really happening was that the clenching of my fists and the pain I felt were reflecting my struggle with God for control over my life.

God's approach to prying my clenched fists open involved making me wait, using both good and bad situations. He began by introducing discomfort within my current ministry roles at the church. Next, He offered new opportunities that excited me but then stalled their progress. He didn't remove them entirely; He just delayed them indefinitely. Then, my wife, who was supposed to die, didn't. That's great, right? It was—but after feeling as though He had gone to great lengths to prepare me for this catastrophic event, it felt anti-climactic for her to keep on living. I even commented to someone once that I wished, if He was going to take her, that He would just hurry up and get it over with so I could move on with my life. Yes, that is as horrible and selfish as it sounds, and I'm dreadfully ashamed of it, but it demonstrates how desperate I was to hang onto control.

Releasing my grip

God wasn't done with me yet. Something I said in a conversation with a colleague was taken out of context and repeated to my boss, who was offended by it. Despite my protests that I had been misquoted and had, for years, demonstrated the opposite attitudes of which I was being accused, my boss believed the false report, and I fell out of favor. Every interaction between us for the two years following that event was clouded by mistrust and suspicion. Systematically, areas of responsibility in which I had excelled were stripped away and given to others. People reporting to me who deserved recognition and promotion were denied promotions, as honoring them might be seen as rewarding my bad behavior.

Slowly, I began to relax my grip as I became aware that dozens of coworkers were watching closely to see how I would respond to the way I was being treated. The person I had the original conversation with had left the company and didn't return my calls, so I had no exculpatory evidence. My colleagues would see right through any self-righteous, passive-aggressive response. Not being in a position to fight, conventional wisdom might suggest that I flee and find another job, but every time I considered that, the Lord made it clear I should stay put. That left me with only one option: waiting.

Being constantly aware that I was living in a glass house, the weight of my waiting took on different characteristics. Instead of feeling the heaviness of frustration, I became conscious of my responsibility to represent Christ well. Rather than being frustrated by the unfair treatment I received, I grew frustrated when I failed to respond to those situations in a Christ-like manner. As I focused on ensuring my attitudes and actions were right before God, He began to open my eyes to see and understand the truths about waiting and hope that I've been sharing here.

Although imperceptibly at first, my heart slowly began to change, and with it, my burden. Its mass did not shrink; in fact, in many ways it grew heavier. The less I focused on how I was treated, the more I became aware of how others were mistreated and my duty to care for and encourage them. The more I chose not to lash out when provoked, the more overt and aggressive the provocations became. The more honest and transparent I aimed to be, the more insidiously and deviously I was betrayed. However, the more I learned to wait patiently, the less heavy the burden felt.

I was being made an example, not by my enemies, but by God—an example of how to behave properly when falsely accused. It was on display for everyone in my life to see, especially at work but also everywhere else. As I focused more and more on ensuring my own actions and motives were upright and pure, I realized I wasn't the real target of the attack; God was. Understanding this allowed me to stop wrestling with waiting. It didn't matter how long the fight took—there was never any doubt who would win it.

Eventually the conflict ended when my position was eliminated and my employment with the company was terminated. That may not sound like a win to you, and in my earlier days of despising waiting and fighting for control, I would have agreed with you. However, it was, in fact, very beneficial for many reasons, not the least of which was that it was an answer to prayer. When I learned to be content with waiting, I simply asked the Lord to clarify how long He wanted me to wait; not because I was eager to leave, but because I was committed to staying as long as He wanted me to. I was so determined to wait that I feared I might miss His instruction to move on if it wasn't clear. Well, when security escorts you out of the building, it doesn't get any clearer than that. It was a win, not because I was vindicated or because the conflict had been resolved in my favor (neither of which occurred), but because, for probably the first time in my life, I had waited well.

I felt like a different person. Making the connection between waiting, hope, and faith radically altered my outlook on life. My perspective on cancer, work, and the lack thereof, on relationships—on everything—changed. Waiting permeated my life, which meant hope was also present everywhere, because you can't have one without the other. And when you have hope—confidence in a God who is real, though unseen, and who can only be and do good—faith becomes easy, as it's the only response that makes sense.

Chapter Five

Hope-driven Waiting

The assault on eagerness

Discovering the synergy between Hebrews 11 and Romans 8 in relation to faith, hope, and waiting was so transformational for me that I became fascinated by the idea that there might be other concepts in Scripture linked to these three that I had previously overlooked. As it turned out, I didn't have to search very far.

> For in hope we have been saved, but hope that is seen is not hope; for who hopes for what he already sees? But if we hope for what we do not see, with perseverance we wait eagerly for it. (Romans 8:24-25)

You may remember a remark I made earlier about having to lump waiting, but that didn't mean I had to like it. That was my attitude for a long time. As it turns out, however, according to Paul, I do have to like it. He says that if I hope for what I do not see, I should wait eagerly for it. I have to admit, eagerness is not typically the emotion

I feel when I'm waiting. If you ask those close to me, they will tell you that I struggle significantly with waiting eagerly. Especially during the time when I was exploring the relationship between hope and waiting, we frequently discussed the fact that I'm really quite bad at it. I understand and accept that waiting and hope go hand in hand, but "eager" is not the word I would choose to describe my usual state of mind while waiting; "reluctant" would be a more accurate choice.

So, I broke out my Greek New Testament along with all my lexicons and study aids to tackle the adverb "eagerly." My aim was to uncover some hidden meaning in the Greek word for "eagerly" that might suggest it conveys something different in Greek than it does in English. Well, folks, the joke was on me. Paul doesn't actually use the Greek word for "eagerly" in Romans 8:25. In fact, he doesn't use any adverb at all. To my chagrin, I discovered that the notion of eagerness is embedded right into the verb "to wait."

Paul had a couple of options in Greek to communicate the idea of waiting. One is *anameno*, a compound word consisting of the preposition *ana* meaning "again," and the verb *meno* meaning "to abide, stay, or remain." This creates the imagery of "staying again" or "remaining again" to convey the concept of waiting. That's how I perceive waiting—just hanging around, again and again, until something happens. It doesn't matter if you're trying to get somewhere or not—you're simply staying put, again and again and again.

Of course, that's not the word Paul chose. Instead, he uses the word *apekdechomai*. Before we look at its etymology, it's interesting to note that of the eight times this word appears in the New Testament, six occur in Paul's writings—seven if you believe he wrote Hebrews. It doesn't seem that he coined the term, as it appears in extra-biblical literature, albeit rarely; however, he certainly was very fond of using it, and he always did so in the context of hope.

Apekdechomai is a compound word made up of two prepositions and a verb. The root verb, *dechomai*, essentially means "to take with the hand." Luke uses *dechomai* when recounting the story of the prophet Simeon, whom the Lord had told would not die before seeing the Messiah. When Joseph and Mary brought the baby Jesus to the temple on the eighth day for his consecration, Luke states that Simeon "took Him into his arms" (Luke 2:28). *Dechomai* does not suggest a rough or aggressive kind of taking; instead, it conveys the gentleness and tender excitement associated with picking up something as delicate as an infant child.

As a result, *dechomai*, eventually came to mean "to receive" or "to welcome," as in welcoming a guest into one's home. It is not a clinical or technical term one would use to describe a business transaction; rather, it is a relational term that conveys warmth and acceptance. It is used in that very fashion in John 4:45, where it is written that when Jesus went to Galilee, "the Galileans received Him, having seen all the things that He did in Jerusalem at the feast," and again in Hebrews 11:31, which describes the faith of Rahab, who "welcomed the spies in peace."

The first of the two prepositions, *ek*, means "out of" or "away from." When compounded with another word, it emphasizes separation. Therefore, when it's added to *dechomai* to form the word *ekdechomai*, it depicts being separated in time from the act of receiving, accepting, or welcoming—in other words, waiting. Due to the positivity and excitement embedded in the concept of *dechomai*, those same emotions are associated with this specific kind of waiting.

In the New Testament, we see that the lame man by the pool of Bethsaida was "waiting for the movement of the waters" (John 5:3) to be the first one in the pool to be healed. After angry Jews forced Paul to flee to Athens, leaving Silas and Timothy behind, Luke says Paul "was waiting" for his friends to join him (Acts 17:16). In English, we express the attitude of *ekdechomai* with phrases like, "I'm looking forward to it," "I can't wait to see you," or "I'm excited for that to happen."

Think again of Simeon. Although Luke doesn't use the term *ekdechomai*, he does use the closely related word *prosdechomai*, which emphasizes anticipation, when he says Simeon was "looking for" the consolation of Israel (Luke 2:25). Simeon had been waiting for years, perhaps most or all of his adult life, for this one moment. Consider how his heart must have skipped a beat each time he saw parents approaching the temple with a newborn babe. Imagine the goosebumps he must have felt every time he heard an infant cry, wondering, "Could this be the one?" Do you think he was disappointed the first hundred times it wasn't the Messiah? Perhaps, but I prefer to think it simply built his excitement for what was to come.

Do you think he got angry with God and accused Him of not loving him, of just toying with his emotions, or of taking delight in frustrating him? Not only could I never imagine Simeon thinking that way, but I also can't see myself feeling that way if I were in his shoes. Nevertheless, even if he occasionally had those thoughts, can't you see how incredibly foolish, petty, and short-sighted they would have been? Yes, Simeon longed for that day, earnestly expected it, and eagerly anticipated it, but he never regretted waiting for it. Put yourself in his position when, as Joseph and Mary entered the temple, the Holy Spirit nudged him and said, "There He is! He's the one! Go ahead—it's okay. Go hold your Messiah, Simeon!" What do you think Simeon's attitude was towards all the waiting he had done in that moment?

With that in mind, let's look at the word Paul uses in Romans 8:25, *apekdechomai*. The preposition, *apo*, also means "out of" or "away from," similar to *ek*. As standalone prepositions, they differ, with *apo* emphasizing "out from the edge of a thing" and *ek* meaning "out from the inside of a thing." When compounded with other words, both convey the notion of separation. Yet, when used together as they are in this case, their redundancy does not reinforce the idea of separation, as one might expect, but instead highlights the expectancy inherent in the concept of *dechomai*, which is why the translators of the NASB render it as "eagerly wait." One of my lexicons describes this kind of waiting as "assiduous,"[26] meaning "dogged and tireless persistence."

Alciphron's puppies

To better visualize what *apekdechomai* waiting looks like, consider an example of its use by Alciphron, a Greek rhetor from the third century AD, when he describes a rabbit hunt. In this passage, *apekdecomai* is translated as "expecting":

> While I was testing the puppies to see whether they were now fit for the chase, I frightened a hare in a thicket, starting her up suddenly; and my sons slipped the puppies from their leashes. The puppies set up a yelping and came near catching the game; but the hare, fleeing from the threat, went over the hillside and found the entrance to a burrow. The keener of the two dogs, with mouth already wide open and expecting every moment to close his jaws upon the prey, went down the hole too, trying to pull out the hare by force, and broke one of his own forelegs.[27]

Can't you feel the excitement of that scene? Can't you see the puppies running with their mouths wide open, tongues flapping in the wind, only to slide their haunches on the grass, legs flailing about in search of traction as the rabbit suddenly changes direction? Can't you sense the energy as one dog launches himself at the rabbit's burrow with such force that he breaks his own leg while dirt flies everywhere? That is the force of *apekdechomai*. That is the picture Paul had in mind when he talked about hope-driven waiting.

Paul says that when we hope for something, we wait for it with the expectancy of a puppy, frantic for the chase and eager in anticipation of chomping down on the prey. It's the excitement of a four-year-old on Christmas Eve, who has just enough experience to know the joy that awaits the next day but is still innocent enough to be surprised by the wonder of it all. It's Simeon-like longing to see and hold the Promised One that he and generations of his ancestors before him had yearned and prayed for. Even though "eagerly" is the best word we have in English to communicate this idea, it somehow doesn't seem to do it justice. This isn't just eagerness—it's eagerness on steroids.

Keep on ticking

As if that were not enough, Paul further describes the posture of hope-driven waiting with the Greek word *hupomone*. About two-thirds of the time it appears in the New Testament, the NASB translates it as "perseverance," and almost all the rest as "endurance." Although several other reputable English translations use the word "patience" or "patiently" in Romans 8:25 and do so appropriately, I believe "perseverance" conveys the intent more accurately and should be preferred. This distinction is important because our English word "patience" and its derivatives are rooted in the Latin word for "suffering," a connotation that pervades our use of them even today.

For example, it is common to say that, as a cancer patient, my wife suffers from cancer. It is cliché to avoid praying for patience, lest the Lord introduce a person or situation into your life that has all the appeal of a porcupine scratching its nails on a blackboard, intent on irritating you to your last nerve. The Greeks had a word to express the act of handling irritants well, *makrothumia*, which the NASB consistently translates as "patience" and means "to be far away or distant from anger," and that the KJV sometimes renders appropriately as "long-suffering." However, that's not the concept Paul wants to communicate here. Instead, he uses *hupomone*, which means "to abide or remain under;" in other words, to be steadfast, to endure, to persevere.

Perseverance is not better than patience or vice versa, nor are they mutually exclusive. In fact, we need both. Paul prayed for the Colossians that they would be "strengthened with all power, according to His glorious might, for the attaining of all steadfastness (*hupomone*) and patience (*makrothumia*)" (Colossians 1:11). However, as we have seen and will continue to see, in passages about hope and waiting, the emphasis is on perseverance, not patience.

Instead of testing your limits to see how long you can tolerate an irritant before getting angry, perseverance is about being built for the long run, able, as they used to say about Timex watches, to "take a licking and keep on ticking." The difference between perseverance and patience lies not in whether bad stuff happens, or how tough they are, but in our attitude and thought processes about them. Patience feels the hurt and chooses not to respond with anger; perseverance absorbs the blow and stays firmly in place. Patience says, "You hurt me, but I don't care." Perseverance says, "I don't care—you can't hurt me."

Paul's combination of *hupomone* and *apekdechomai* in the context of hope is pure genius. Perseverance naturally goes hand-in-hand with the eager expectation of hope. When you are excitedly waiting for something you hope for, you don't patiently suffer through the experience; you hardly feel it at all. If you are truly convinced of God's goodness and confident in the reality of His promises, even when you haven't seen them yet, how can you wait with any other attitude than, "Bring it on! Do what you will—nothing will stop God from being good and keeping His promises. I don't care what happens in between or how long it takes; it's all over but the shouting."

Genesis 29:20 tells us that the seven years Jacob worked for Rachel seemed like only a few days to him. That's what eagerly waiting with perseverance looks like, and that's how we're supposed to wait. Remember that Laban, Jacob's father-in-law, was self-serving, deceitful, and conniving—not a pleasant man to work for. However, because of how much Jacob loved Rachel and his hope of marrying her, all of Laban's nonsense simply didn't faze him.

The Waiting Wheel

Associating the concepts of eager anticipation and perseverance with hope and faith has unlocked a completely new perspective on waiting for me. It has enabled me to see a pattern—an engine of sorts—that is expressly taught twice in the New Testament and illustrated or referenced in numerous other places. Within this pattern lie the keys to understanding how God designed waiting to work, why we struggle with it so much, and where its weight comes from. More importantly, it helps us identify what we need to do to realign our hearts and minds when our waiting feels more characterized by dread and failure than by eager anticipation and perseverance.

The first of these two passages is James 1:2-4.

> Consider it all joy, my brethren, when you encounter various trials, knowing that the testing of your faith produces endurance. And let endurance have its perfect result, so that you may be perfect and complete, lacking in nothing.

Here we see that James presents perseverance as part of a formulaic progression of ideas. Perseverance serves both as a product and as an input to other concepts. In a more graphical format, James first states that:

FAITH + TESTING → PERSEVERANCE

Hebrews 11 teaches us that faith has component parts, specifically that it is action based on hope. We can add that concept to our diagram, chaining the two together.

HOPE + ACTION → FAITH + TESTING → PERSEVERANCE

Hebrews 11 also teaches us that hope is confidence in an unseen reality. This unseen reality is nothing less than God Himself, and our confidence rests in His character, specifically that He is good.

CHARACTER + CONFIDENCE → HOPE + ACTION → FAITH + TESTING → PERSEVERANCE

A key idea highlighted by mapping these relationships in this fashion is that perseverance isn't something simply given to us; it's the product of the interaction between testing and our faith. Perseverance isn't an inert resource sitting in one of God's storehouses for Him to dole out as needed or requested; it arises from faith being tested. Perseverance is a by-product, just like we learned in basic chemistry, where salt, water, and heat are produced when an acid is mixed with a base. Perseverance doesn't occur naturally; it must be manufactured.

In fact, when Paul prays for the church in Colossians 1:9, he doesn't ask that they be filled with perseverance and patience, as he does for knowledge, wisdom, and understanding. Certainly, it cannot be more challenging for God to dispense perseverance than it is for Him to grant understanding. It isn't, or it wouldn't be, if it were not for the fact that He didn't design perseverance to work that way. Instead, Paul prays that the Colossians will be strengthened with the power of God's might so that they can attain perseverance and patience (Colossians 1:11), because he knows they must be produced, and that the only way that happens is through testing faith.

Additionally, despite the discomfort surrounding the very idea of testing, understanding this progression gives meaning and purpose to waiting. Waiting was not designed to inflict the weight of pointlessness. When approached correctly, it produces something valuable. Remember that waiting is itself a by-product of time, created by God for the specific purpose of establishing our relationship with Him on the foundation of faith, which only exists when it is exercised. The beauty in all of this is that waiting, hope, faith, and testing are not ends in themselves, nor is the effort devoted to them wasted. They have a by-product: they produce perseverance.

It doesn't stop there, either. Look at what James says next.

> And let endurance have its perfect result, so that you may be perfect and complete, lacking in nothing. (James 1:4)

The word "perfect," used twice in this verse, does not mean "without blemish or flaw" as we would naturally assume. Instead, it signifies "finished," in the sense of having achieved a goal. The word "complete" means "whole or entire." Additionally, perseverance is not merely an end goal; it also yields something more. The by-product of perseverance is a whole, complete, and entirely finished you. Ultimately, perseverance leads to maturity.

What does maturity mean, and what does it look like? Paul tells us that in Ephesians 4:13:

> until we all attain to the unity of the faith, and of the knowledge of the Son of God, to a mature man, to the measure of the stature which belongs to the fullness of Christ.

In other words, the goal of this entire process is to make me like Jesus. The perfect result of *hupomone*—endurance, perseverance—is to produce the character of God within me.

Note that just as the full measure of perseverance isn't achieved in one go, neither is maturity in Christ. Both require repetition. This means that testing must occur repeatedly. Admittedly, that's not an appealing idea for any of us, including James himself and the original recipients of his letter. We will examine how James addresses this issue shortly, but for now, we must recognize that repetition is inherent in and integral to the process. This is important because it helps us see that the benefits of both perseverance and maturity are cumulative. The testing of my faith yesterday produced perseverance that created the foundation for the testing of my faith today, which in turn will form the basis for the perseverance that will emerge when my faith is tested tomorrow.

This is where our discussion in the last chapter about God's intentional design of encapsulating the entire universe in time and declaring it to be good hits home in a somber way. We would all agree that spiritual maturity is good. We would also unanimously agree that perseverance is good. We can likely even convince ourselves that the testing of our faith is good—at least from time to time. However, what troubles us is the seemingly incessant barrage of trials. How many times have you said or thought, "What now, Lord? Why can't I catch a break? Why does everything bad happen at once? What do I have to do to find some relief?"

At the heart of complaints like these is the notion that experiencing trials repeatedly is bad. However, the repetitive testing of our faith is essential for cultivating perseverance and ultimately achieving Christlike maturity. Why? Because God designed it that way. When God created time, He not only created waiting, but also created repetition. He made it integral to every growth cycle, be it physical, intellectual, social, emotional, or spiritual. And when He declared time to be good, He also deemed the repetition in those cycles to be good.

Look at what happens when we add these concepts to our diagram.

Do you see how beautiful the pattern is that emerges? Confidence in the character of God, especially His goodness, embodies hope. Acting on hope reflects faith, which must undergo testing. The testing of faith produces perseverance, which, when repeated over time produces Christlikeness—the character of God in us. This, in turn, leads to greater confidence, bolder actions, and the ability to withstand more intense testing, establishing the foundation necessary to repeat the cycle at a higher level. It is the engine that powers our spiritual growth. Its design is stunningly simple yet marvelously intricate in its ramifications. At the core of all this is waiting, constructed against the backdrop of time and beautifully permeating every aspect.

The part I don't like

What doesn't seem so beautiful in the pattern that James presents are the "trials" and "testing" he talks about. He clearly views them as not only beneficial but also necessary to the whole engine, so they warrant closer scrutiny. The two terms are conceptually related, yet they stem from different Greek root words. The first thing to note is that the phrase "various trials" in James 1:2 is intentionally broad and generic. The Greek word for "trial," *peirasmos*, can refer to any kind of test with any kind of intention. When used positively, it can imply a sincere desire to prove the genuineness of something or to confirm its validity; in a negative context, it may represent a threat or overt attempt to mislead or cause failure.

By modifying it further with the word "various" (literally, "multi-colored"), James underscores that "trials" can encompass absolutely anything. They can be morally neutral, varying in significance from inconsequential matters like your favorite flavor of ice cream being discontinued to life-altering events such as being laid off without warning. Trials can also arise from our own desires (James 1:14), from other people (Matthew 16:1), or even from the devil himself (Luke 4:1-12). Additionally, they may be events orchestrated by God to validate or strengthen faith (John 6:6). The only caveat, as James carefully reminds us in verses 13-14, is that God does not tempt anyone to sin. Beyond that, the concept of what defines a trial is quite broad and inclusive.

The word for "testing" in James 1:3, *dokimion*, is more restrictive, and indicates something that has been proven or accepted following examination or trial. What is particularly interesting for us is that it is a noun form of our old friend *dechomai*, which conveys the idea of being accepted as good, valid, or true.

What we can infer from the definitions of "trials" and "testing" is that, while the source and nature of the trial can be virtually anything, the act of being tested alone does not produce perseverance. Perseverance is only cultivated when faith is proven to be genuine. So, how do we know if faith is authentic? We see it when, in the middle of a trial, a person acts in a way that aligns with his hope and unwavering conviction in the goodness of God and His promises. If that person doesn't act in faith during the trial, it does not lead to perseverance, which means that person is not maturing in Christlikeness. James illustrates this principle in verses 5-7, where he discusses requests for wisdom. If a man asks in faith, he will receive wisdom; but if he asks with doubt, he not only does not receive the wisdom he asked for, but he also becomes even more confused.

The other Scripture passage where this progression is explicitly laid out for us is Romans 5:2-5:

> And not only this, but we also exult in our tribulations, knowing that tribulation brings about perseverance; and perseverance, proven character; and proven character, hope; and hope

does not disappoint, because the love of God has been poured out within our hearts through the Holy Spirit who was given to us.

The parallelism between these verses and James 1:1-4 is impossible to miss. While Paul does not explicitly mention that our faith is tested in our tribulations, it's inferred by the fact that the result is the same: *hupomone*, the same word found in James 1:3. Moreover, the word translated "brings about" in Romans 5:2 is identical to the one rendered "produces" in James 1:3. Finally, even though they don't use identical words, the "proven character" Paul refers to correlates with the maturity ("perfect and complete") that James describes. In fact, the Greek word for "proven character" is *dokime*, which derives from *dechomai*, as does *dokimion*, the word for "testing" in James 1:3.

The fact that two different biblical authors present the exact same sequence not only underscores its importance but also amplifies our understanding of it. For example, while James leaves us to infer the cyclical nature of the maturation process, Paul points it out directly by highlighting that character produces hope.

Hope doesn't disappoint

Paul tells us something else about hope that's very important. As I observed at the beginning of this book, for hope to be meaningful, it must be real. It needs to make a difference. It needs to work every time, everywhere, and in every situation, without exception. This is exactly what Paul says biblical hope promises.

> and hope does not disappoint, because the love of God has been poured out within our hearts through the Holy Spirit

who was given to us. For while we were still helpless, at the right time Christ died for the ungodly. (Romans 5:5-6)

Biblical hope doesn't disappoint. It never lets us down. Never. It never gives us reason to be disillusioned or ashamed that we relied on it. Not ever. Not a single time. Hope doesn't disappoint because God is our hope, and He never disappoints. We have His personal promise and guarantee on that. Notice the reference to all three persons of the Godhead in the verses above. The love of the Father, the Son's sacrifice, and the gift of the Holy Spirit are proof that hope in Him is the surest of sure things. Consider what Paul says just before discussing our waiting wheel.

> Therefore, having been justified by faith, we have peace with God through our Lord Jesus Christ, through whom also we have obtained our introduction by faith into this grace in which we stand; and we exult in hope of the glory of God. (Romans 5:1)

It's one thing to believe something; it's another to brag about it. According to Paul, our reason for boasting is our absolute conviction (or hope) in the glory of God. This is no small thing. God is extremely jealous of His glory. He takes it very seriously—so seriously, in fact, that of all the wonderful things He gives us, His glory is the one thing He doesn't share with anyone (Isaiah 42:8). So, when He stakes His name and reputation, it's a big deal, and that's exactly what Romans 5:5-6 says He has done.

Notice how tightly connected this is to our justification. The same level of guarantee that God gives us regarding our salvation is the same level of guarantee that He provides to assure us that the hope based on His character will not disappoint. The love God has poured into our hearts through the Holy Spirit because of the sacrifice of Jesus Christ not only gives us confidence in a future home in heaven, but it also enables us to view our tribulations through a radically new lens. To help us gain this perspective on testing—and, by extension, waiting—we need to examine what James has to say on the topic.

The work of joy

James suggests that our attitude towards trials and testing should be one of joy. Interestingly, neither he nor Paul presents joy as a component of spiritual growth, whether as an input or an output, as they do with faith and perseverance, despite its prominent presence in both passages. Paul says that joy is part of the evidence that we are walking in the Spirit (Galatians 5:22), and John implies that joy will characterize our eternal state in the new heavens and earth (Revelation 21:4). However, there is no indication that perseverance or maturity produces joy. James also does not imply that waiting, hope, faith, or perseverance are triggered by joy. Instead, he simply gives a directive: "Consider it all joy, my brethren, when you encounter various trials" (James 1:2).

Positioning joy as a choice rather than an input or output of a process, like perseverance, frustrates me and runs counter to the way we think about and want waiting to work. Because I dislike waiting, I'm uncomfortable with the idea of being told to be happy while doing so. I would rather reserve the right to express whatever emotion I find suitable during a challenging situation and afterward, depending on my perspective on the outcome. Most of the time, I'm totally OK with positive results making me happy, but I believe I should have the leeway to not be pleased when things don't go or turn out as I believe they should. James, however, doesn't offer any such wiggle room.

The Greek word for "consider," *hegeomai*, paints an interesting word picture. It comes from a root meaning "to lead," and its primary meaning is "to rule or lead." This meaning appears twice in Matthew 2:6 when the chief priests quote the prophet Micah about the Messiah's birthplace, stating that Bethlehem is not the least among the "leaders of Judah" and that from it will come "a ruler who will shepherd my people, Israel." This is also the word Jesus uses when He teaches that, in the kingdom of God, the "leader" must become like the servant (Luke 22:26). Additionally, it is the word Stephen uses to describe Joseph when Pharaoh appointed him as "governor over Egypt and all his household" (Acts 7:10). The noun forms are used to identify princes, rulers, and governors, along with their reigns (Luke 20:20, Mark 13:9, 1 Peter 2:14, Luke 3:1).

By extension, when *hegeomai* is used to describe a thought process or attitude, as in James 1:2, that thought should be the governing principle of one's mindset. Paul explicitly uses it in this sense when he says that our attitudes toward others should be governed by "regarding" them as more important than ourselves, because Jesus did not "regard" His equality with God as something to be held onto (Philippians 2:3-6). Later in that same letter, he declares that he "counts" everything that should have been an advantage to him as rubbish compared to what he has in Christ (Philippians 3:7-8). He also instructs Timothy to tell slaves that their disposition toward their masters should be to "regard" them as worthy of all honor (1 Timothy 6:1). "Consider" is unaffected by outcomes, feelings, or relative situations. Instead, it establishes an inviolable fundamental operating principle that remains true and governs my behavior irrespective of results, emotions, or circumstances.

In 2014, the Yale Center for Faith & Culture at Yale Divinity School published a series of interviews as part of a project titled

Theology of Joy & the Good Life. They asked renown thinkers in the fields of theology, philosophy, economics, psychology, and music to explain their perspective on joy and how it influences their respective disciplines. The results were eclectic, as you might imagine, with some ideas even being somewhat contradictory at times. While none of the individuals interviewed directly referenced Scripture to support their views, several of their observations resonated as true, including one by Willie James Jennings, associate professor of Systematic Theology and Africana Studies at Yale, who said, "Joy is a work that can become a state, that can become a way of life."[28]

By instructing his readers to "consider it all joy," I believe James was attempting to convey exactly that. Given as a command, James directs us to do a work, namely, to consciously establish joy as the governing principle of our mindset and attitude toward trials, aiming to make it our way of life, which will eventually evoke an emotional response. The use of the imperative means that this is primarily an act of will. While joy can appear as an emotional response of elation, happiness, and gratitude, it is essentially a deliberate choice to prioritize God and the work He is doing to conform us into the image of His Son above all else, and to celebrate every opportunity He takes to advance that cause.

Jesus takes it even further. He says, "Blessed are you when people insult you and persecute you, and falsely say all kinds of evil against you because of Me. Rejoice and be glad, for your reward in heaven is great; for in the same way they persecuted the prophets who were before you" (Matthew 5:11-12). In addition to restating the command to rejoice amid trials, He directly ties it to hope ("your reward in heaven") and blessing, which implies that an attitude of joy in testing also results in an expansion and reinforcement of hope.

Once again, let me emphasize that this does not mean we should rejoice in evil things. In fact, passages like 1 Corinthians 13:6 and

Proverbs 2:10-15 explicitly teach against that. This does not deny that genuinely bad things exist and happen. When an eight-year-old girl, sitting at her kitchen table doing her homework, is killed by a stray bullet from a gang-related drive-by shooting in front of her house, that is not good. It is horrible, evil, and tragic, and no one is saying that should be a cause for rejoicing—not James, not Paul, not Jesus, not I. However, events like that give us the opportunity to respond in faith, to take action based on hope. When we do that, perseverance is produced, and we grow in Christ, which is something to celebrate.

Paul presents the same idea from a different perspective. The Greek word translated as "exult" in Romans 5 means "to boast or brag." Whether bragging is seen as good or bad depends on its use and context; in this case, it's obviously positive and something to celebrate. When your faith is tested, it's an indication that there's something valuable worth testing, regardless of whether the adversary is trying to disprove it, or the Father is looking to confirm and validate it. Paul says that's reason for bragging and shows us how to do it. Speaking of his infamous "thorn in the flesh," which the Lord refused to remove despite his repeated requests, he said, "Most gladly, therefore, I will rather boast about my weaknesses, so that the power of Christ may dwell in me" (2 Corinthians 12:9).

Real-world proof

While diagramming these concepts helps us visualize and internalize their relationships, it can also make them seem sterile. They may be interesting to think about, but do they actually present a practical, real-world, hands-in-the-dirt way to live life? The author of Hebrews thought so. Although he doesn't lay things out as crisply as we see in James and Romans, he does apply all the concepts we've discussed to the very real challenges his readers faced.

Hope-driven Waiting

As you will recall, the original recipients of his letter were in a bad way. Facing oppression from the Roman government, excommunication from the Jewish synagogue, and contradictory teachings from heretical Judaizers, they were under extraordinary pressure to abandon their faith and turn back. As their conflict and confusion grew, so did their fear; and their fear, in the words of Scot Pollok, was beginning to cause them to step back and curl up.

Even though the reasons for and nature of the conflict, confusion, pain, and waiting in your life may differ from those of first-century Jewish believers, you can undoubtedly identify with their feelings and state of mind. Whether you find yourself in such a place right now or have in the past, I'm sure you are all too familiar with the feeling of being overwhelmed, of feeling trapped between the proverbial rock and a hard place, wondering if there will ever come a time when your back won't be breaking under the weight, and whether believing in God actually matters. I'm sure you know what it's like for fear and anxiety to cause your faith to step back and curl up, because I do. I've been there, you've been there, and that's exactly where the original recipients of this letter found themselves.

With that perspective in mind, it is clear that Hebrews 10:38-39 is the focal point toward which the author has been building the entire book.

> BUT MY RIGHTEOUS ONE SHALL LIVE BY FAITH;
>
> AND IF HE SHRINKS BACK, MY SOUL HAS NO PLEASURE IN HIM.
>
> But we are not of those who shrink back to destruction, but of those who have faith to the preserving of the soul. (Hebrews 10:38-39)

Over the centuries, many have erroneously attempted to use this idea of shrinking back to claim that it is possible for a person to lose their salvation. Not only does that notion directly contradict clear teaching in many other parts of Scripture, but it also completely misinterprets or ignores the immediate context of verses 32-36, which highlight the challenges faced by those Jewish believers, as I just described. This passage is not about losing our righteous standing before God; rather, it addresses the reality of fear-inducing circumstances that lead us to want to shrink back—to step back, curl up, and hide.

Since we've already unpacked the keywords and concepts in this passage, we won't rehash the details. However, I challenge you to read Hebrews 10:32—11:39 again, this time paying attention to the words and rationale the author uses to encourage those who want to shrink back.

The language of hope should explode off the page at you. Perseverance. Confidence. Receiving what was promised. The goodness of God. Testing. Faith. Hope. Waiting. Lots of waiting. He cites 18 specific examples of people who, convinced of God's goodness and His promises, acted in faith, had that faith tested, and persevered. He then mentions six others by name without describing their stories and describes numerous forms of persecution without naming names. The faces and situations may change, but the pattern remains the same. No matter how often the cycle is repeated, the result never changes. Waiting and conviction of God's goodness produce hope. Hope leads to faith, which when tested produces perseverance, which produces character, which produces hope. And hope never disappoints.

I hate when Hebrews 11 is called the "Hall of Faith" and those mentioned there are referred to as "heroes," because it suggests that it's like our Halls of Fame, where only the best of the best are honored. We hold those memorialized in such spaces with such reverence that the buildings are often seen as sacred shrines. That's the farthest thing from the author's intention. His whole point is that these people weren't extraordinary; they weren't the strongest or the best of the best. They were normal John and Jane Does, just like you and me. After all, how many women have you ever met named Rahab? No one wants to name their daughter after a prostitute. I've met some Delilahs, but never a Rahab, yet she's included on this list. Speaking of Delilah, have you read Samson's story honestly and objectively lately? He had his moments, but most of the time he was a selfish, womanizing fool—yet he's mentioned, too. Don't even get me started on Jephthah. Read his story in Judges 11 and 12 if you're not familiar with it and let me know if you think he should be heralded as a "hero of faith." If the goal was to list the elite, having Jephthah named while men like Job, Isaiah, and Daniel get only veiled references would make this so-called hall a complete travesty.

The people named and referenced in Hebrews 11 were not models of perfect, unassailable character—far from it. They were flawed, many of them severely so, which is what makes their stories incredibly relevant, because you and I are just as flawed as they were. What they have in common is that, despite their imperfections, they waited, hoped, and acted in faith. When their faith was tested, they persevered and grew. They are included in this list not because they had arrived but precisely because they hadn't. Because they were as imperfect as you and I are, the author wants to encourage us to follow their example and leave us without any excuse for not acting in faith ourselves.

However, the message is not simply "if they did it, you can do it, too," but rather, "the process worked for them, so it will work for you, too." In fact, the author emphasizes that even these so-called giants of faith, like Moses, Abraham, and Enoch, haven't completely arrived yet.

> And all these, having gained approval through their faith, did not receive what was promised, because God had provided something better for us, so that apart from us they would not be made perfect. (Hebrews 11:39-40)

They gained approval, but they still aren't complete. God has something much greater in mind, and He's holding it in reserve for the day when all His children, from Adam onward, can enjoy it together. Do you know what that means? Moses, Abraham, Enoch, and all the others are still waiting. That's not just a curious quirk in God's plan; it's actually essential and extremely important. As long as everyone is still waiting, there is still hope. You can't have one without the other, remember? If Abraham had completely received the promise, if he had already been made complete, hope would be gone, not just for him but for the rest of us too.

I can't speak for you, but realizing I can gain approval like Enoch did without walking straight into the Lord's presence as he did puts a little more pep in my step. Knowing that even the Apostle Paul, who instructed us to follow him as he followed Christ, isn't perfect, allows my tongue to wag a little more like Alciphron's puppies. I'm beginning to understand why Paul was such a big fan of the word *apekdechomai* and why he knew no other way to hope. When you start to grasp how significant that day will be when we are all made perfect together, eager anticipation is the only response that makes sense.

Is that truly relevant to the grind of everyday life? Even if your world resembles a clichéd, country music ballad, where you've lost your job, your woman, and your truck; where your best friend betrayed you, your dog hates you, and you can't even afford a beer to drown your sorrows, I say yes. The author of Hebrews says yes. God says yes. Focusing on the hope of promises yet to come realigns our perspective on everything in between now and then. It alters priorities and fundamentally changes what we value and the weight we assign to our burdens. Jesus put it this way:

> "I say to you, My friends, do not be afraid of those who kill the body and after that have no more that they can do. But I will warn you whom to fear: fear the One who, after He has killed, has authority to cast into hell; yes, I tell you, fear Him! Are not five sparrows sold for two cents? Yet not one of them is forgotten before God. Indeed, the very hairs of your head are all numbered. Do not fear; you are more valuable than many sparrows." (Luke 12:4-7)

Jesus wasn't diminishing the meaning of life or belittling the reality of death. He was saying that even if your enemies do their worst and kill you, the thing you need to be concerned about is your relationship with God. Being killed by someone isn't the worst thing that can happen. Facing a holy Judge without the protection of Christ's redemptive work is. All other concerns—health issues, financial struggles, relationship problems—pale in comparison.

Therefore, when I recognize that I'm not eagerly waiting with perseverance, I understand that's a warning light, a check engine indicator, if you will, for my hope. It means that my perspective is out of whack, that I am worrying about something I should not be worrying about, and that what I say I believe isn't aligned with the way I'm thinking or acting.

The goodness of discipline

This is a difficult concept to wrap our heads and hearts around. The author seems to realize this, because he directs our attention to one last example of faith: Jesus Himself.

> Therefore, since we have so great a cloud of witnesses surrounding us, let us also lay aside every encumbrance and the sin which so easily entangles us, and let us run with endurance the race that is set before us, fixing our eyes on Jesus, the author and perfecter of faith, who for the joy set before Him endured the cross, despising the shame, and has sat down at the right hand of the throne of God. For consider Him who has endured such hostility by sinners against Himself, so that you will not grow weary and lose heart. (Hebrews 12:1-3)

To ensure we're not applying this passage out of context, let's review it quickly to make sure it contains all the elements we've been discussing.

Some are easy to identify. The words "joy," "faith," and "perseverance" are used explicitly. Others are clearly present, albeit mentioned indirectly. The phrase "set before" appears twice and speaks of hope, as does "despising the shame," which echoes the idea of hope not disappointing from Romans 5:5. The references to testing are rather obvious: "every encumbrance," "sin which so easily entangles us," "shame," and "hostility."

The rest are somewhat more challenging to see, yet they remain apparent. Verse 2 says that "for the joy set before Him," Jesus "endured the cross." This is action rooted in hope. The reference to proven character arises from the fact that Jesus is the "perfecter" of faith, the same word used in James 1:4 as the by-product of perseverance. The element of time is captured in the word "run." The Greek word used here is the root of our English word "trek." This is not a sprint; it is a long-distance race and covering long distances takes time. We also see references to time in verse 3, "Him who has endured." This is the verb form of *hupomone*, perseverance, which, as previously mentioned, suggests the passage of time and waiting. Additionally, the particular form used here, called a perfect participle, indicates a completed action with continuing results, meaning that Jesus continues to endure hostility from sinners to this day, despite having been crucified only once. This not only provides a reference to time but also highlights the repetitive nature of trials.

So, there we have everything. We have all the elements in the model—except one. Where is the goodness of God?

Ironically, wasn't that the question at the heart of these Jewish believers facing their challenges? Isn't that the question central to your struggles with waiting and hope? I know it is for me.

As it turns out, the goodness of God is present in Hebrews 12, but to see how, we have to look at verses 7-10.

> It is for discipline that you endure; God deals with you as with sons; for what son is there whom his father does not discipline? But if you are without discipline, of which all have become partakers, then you are illegitimate children and not sons. Furthermore, we had earthly fathers to discipline us, and we respected them; shall we not much rather be subject to the Father of spirits, and live? For they disciplined us for a short time as seemed best to them, but He disciplines us for our good, so that we may share His holiness. (Hebrews 12:7-10)

You see, the goodness of God is not merely a part of the process of waiting, hoping, believing, testing, enduring, and maturing. The process itself—the whole experience—is the goodness of God. The author refers to it as *paideia*: discipline, training, and child-rearing. It's how you know you are a child of God and that He loves you; He invests the time and care to help you grow and mature. It's not that He loves those who are not His children any less, but when it comes to spiritual growth, this process simply cannot work for someone who isn't His child. Remember the lesson from Enoch? "He who comes to God must believe that He is and that He is a rewarder of those who seek Him" (Hebrews 11:6). If you don't approach God and His discipline with the expectation that He is good, the process will not function effectively, because there is no faith to validate. However, when we engage with discipline, understanding that He is good, then the training itself becomes beneficial, knowing He is doing it for our good.

Furthermore, His goal in disciplining us is for us to share in His holiness—that His character may be duplicated and demonstrated in ours. When Jesus endured the cross, He proved the character of God, showing not only that He loved us (Romans 5:8), but that He is both "just and the justifier of the one who has faith in Jesus" (Romans 3:26). When we follow His example, the character of God is proven and manifested in us.

Granted, discipline never feels good in the moment, but when we allow ourselves to be trained by it, we see results, and that's when we begin to appreciate it (Hebrews 12:11). Just because you feel pain doesn't mean you've lost hope. Experiencing the weight of waiting is not a character flaw. However, when those challenges cause you to shrink back and curl up, making you want to give up and revert to trying to control your life, you've lost perspective.

Therefore, discipline is not just a description of the process; it's the attitude with which we should approach the process. This is what the author conveys when he says that *hupomone*, or enduring and persevering, represents discipline. Understanding that God's goal is to produce His character within me shifts how I perceive the waiting, pain, and burdens that come with testing. If I lose sight of that goal, I will shy away from what is meant to benefit me and instead cling to things that weigh me down. However, fostering a disciplined mindset counters my tendency to focus on the short-term pain in favor of long-term gain.

Chapter Six

Waiting Well

How do I wait well?

With all due respect to James, Paul, and the author of Hebrews, as wonderful as these concepts are, they sound like work, don't they? Testing, trials, and tribulations are hard things. It's one thing to want to wait eagerly, to intend to make joy the driving principle of your life, and to talk about boasting in hope; it's something completely different to actually do it.

The more I read about these things in the Bible and the more I studied them, the more excited I became about what living life that way could look like. However, as I tried to put them into practice, my results were less than optimal. I would express my confidence in the goodness of God one moment and then worry about how we would pay a medical bill the next. I would endure steadily through one of Crystal's week-long hospitalizations, only to snap at her impatiently when she interrupted whatever I was doing to ask me to carry a load of laundry or empty a trash can. Even when I became more comfortable with the idea that waiting would be an ever-present part of my life and that it was good, I knew my execution wasn't on par with my understanding. I wasn't concerned about whether God was frustrated with me; I was frustrated with myself enough for both of us.

The hardest part for me was waiting with eagerness. Even when I approached challenging events and people in my life with hope and did the right things, acting in faith, there was no eagerness in it. I knew I should be experiencing joy, but the closest I seemed to get was a sense of content acceptance. There was no *apekdechomai*, no tongue flapping in the wind, no frothing at the mouth, no eager anticipation of the opportunity to wait. Instinctively, I described my struggle to my friends in these terms: I was learning to wait, but I wasn't waiting well.

"What does waiting well even mean?" several of them asked. At first, I didn't have a good answer for them. I'd given a lot of thought to many aspects of waiting, but that wasn't one of them. Somehow, however, it began to register with me that waiting is not just something that passively happens to us or merely a context in which we exist; it's a skill that can be learned, improved, and mastered. Intuitively, I recognized that I needed to get better at waiting, but I wasn't completely sure what "better" looked like, and I was even less confident about how to make it happen. As I meditated on these issues to provide my friends with an answer to their question, I began to realize that maybe I had a better understanding than I thought.

Putting the scissors down

As I've mentioned before, this perspective on waiting and hope did not come to me overnight. The Lord has helped me grow into it over time, stretching me in certain areas for a while, allowing some things to simmer in the background while He actively taught me others, only to eventually revisit some of the old lessons and stretch me further. One tool He has consistently used throughout this process is the teaching and insight of others. When it came to understanding what waiting well looked like, help arrived in the form of Russell Johnson, the teaching pastor of my local church.

While working through a series on Genesis 1-3, Russell spent a sermon discussing the seventh day of creation—the Sabbath. He emphasized that the word "Sabbath" means to cease, to stop, or, in his words, "shut it down." He pointed out that Genesis 2:1-3 indicates that God stopped working because His work was complete. "Why does God stop [His work]? . . . It says twice that God completed it . . . If there is ever a time to stop doing something, it is when the work is done, when it is all over . . . It's like a good barber—they know when to put the scissors down."[29]

The image of a barber resonated with me in several ways. First, the analogy of a barber knowing when to stop cutting is particularly poignant. Any skill that involves cutting or chipping away, such as sculpting, carving, or cutting hair, demands both a precise and delicate touch, along with a keen eye to recognize when enough is enough. Once the material is removed, there's no way to put it back. Knowing when to stop often makes the difference between a masterpiece and a disaster.

Russell's word picture resonated with me in another way as well. Until my youngest son, Drew, was in grade school, he would throw a temper tantrum anytime I tried to cut his hair. He would kick, scream, and thrash about so much that giving him a decent haircut was both challenging and dangerous. Eventually I resorted to taking him to a hair salon, and holding him in my lap, arms wrapped tightly around him to keep him still, while someone else did the actual haircut. Russell's analogy made me realize that I accept waiting the same way Drew took a haircut. In these seasons of waiting, I wrestle, I kick, and I scream, acting as though I were being tortured. Like a toddler writhing in a tantrum, I lose the ability to focus on anything besides what I think will bring an end to my ordeal.

Russell then pointed out that the word translated as "rested" twice in Genesis 2:2-3 is *shabath*, or sabbath, but in Exodus 20:11, when explaining the rationale for the fourth commandment, the word for "rested" is *nuach*, which means "to kick back and settle in." It's not the idea of recovery from exertion, as we typically think of rest, but rather the notion that we're just going to relax and hang out here for a while, not because we're tired, but because the work is done. In fact, Russell believes that the absence of the phrase "and the evening and the morning were the seventh day" indicates that God intended to "settle in and dwell with His creation, and it would be great and perfect. It would have no end—the seventh day would have no end."[30]

Finding a place for rest

The words Russell used triggered a chain reaction in my brain. "Shut it down" sounds a lot like waiting. So does the phrase "no end." It would be "perfect," and God's work was "complete." James uses the same terminology, terminology that we have connected to time and repetition. Even the omission of "the evening and the morning" from the account of the seventh day highlights a reference to time by its absence. Of course—it made such perfect sense that I wondered how I could have possibly overlooked it previously. The seventh day is about rest, and rest is connected to time and waiting, just like hope and faith.

The curious thing was that while the idea of rest was obviously related to all the other concepts associated with waiting I'd been exploring, it wasn't clear where it belonged. James makes no mention of rest in his epistle, either directly or indirectly. Neither does Paul in either Romans 5 or 8. You would think that with all the turmoil and confusion facing Jewish believers, if the idea of rest was as closely connected as it seemed, there would be some mention of it in Hebrews, but . . . wait a second. Rest *is* discussed in Hebrews. In fact, there are two whole chapters dedicated to it. Could it be that the connection I was looking for was there?

I reviewed Hebrews 3 and 4 for repeated words and concepts to determine their relevance to the topics we've been studying. The first term I noticed was the one that brought me here in the first place: rest. It occurs 12 times in the 35 combined verses of these two chapters. The word "hope" appears just once, but when you add the instances of "assurance," "confidence," and "promise," there are a total of five hope-related words. Variations of "faith" show up four times. There are six references to trials and testing. Although "perseverance" is not mentioned, "hold fast" appears three times. The words "day" and "today," which reference time, are used ten times. There's even a direct mention of God finishing His work.

They seem pretty relevant to me.

As I've mentioned several times, the issue the author addresses is the instinct of his readers to shrink back and return to their old ways because of the intense pressure and persecution they were facing. He tackles that mindset from various angles throughout the book. In this section, he's specifically countering the teachings of the Judaizers, who claimed that to be right with God, one must not only believe in Jesus but also adhere to the law of Moses. He uses the concept of Sabbath rest to establish two points. The first is the same point Russell made from Genesis 2:13: God rested because He completed His work, inviting us into that rest by believing in

His finished work (Hebrews 4:3-4). The second point is that if you insist on continuing to work, you haven't entered into rest, meaning you don't believe (Hebrews 3:18). The question before us, however, is a bit different. What does it mean to wait well, and how can I improve at it? Without violating the original context and message of the passage, let's see what these two chapters in Hebrews have to say about that.

The answer to what it means to wait well can be difficult to discern from this passage because the author uses a teaching technique familiar to Middle Eastern 1st-century Jews but does not resonate as clearly with our Western 21st century Gentile brains. Instead of defining rest and waiting well is, he describes, quite repetitively, what it is not.

Massah and Meribah

The basis of the argument in Hebrews 3 and 4 is Psalm 95, which refers to an event that happened at a place called Massah and Meribah. According to records in Exodus and Numbers, approximately 2-3 months after being liberated from their bondage in Egypt, the children of Israel arrived at a place identified as Rephidim on their way to Canaan, the land God had promised them. The exact location of Rephidim is unknown, but many believe it was in the region of modern-day Wadi Feiran, a large, fertile valley in the southwestern portion of the Sinai Peninsula. They clearly expected to find water there, but for some undocumented reason, there was none, leading the people to quarrel against Moses (Exodus 17:2). This was no minor complaint. Moses feared for his life, convinced the people were about to stone him (Exodus 17:4). God instructed Moses to strike a rock at the base of Mt. Horeb, which he did, and it poured out enough water to satisfy not only 2-3 million disgruntled people but also all their livestock. Exodus 17:7 records that

> He named the place Massah and Meribah because of the quarrel of the sons of Israel, and because they tested the LORD, saying, "Is the LORD among us, or not?"

It was common for people to assign names to places to commemorate important events that happened there, but the fact that Moses gave the place two names is both unusual and significant. These names speak volumes about the intensity and nature of the emotions expressed in this conflict. Meribah means "place of quarrel" and reflects the people's perspective on the issue. We often see quarrels as heated arguments over trivial things, but the situation was anything but trivial in the eyes of the Israelites.

The text does not specify why the lack of water at Rephidim led to such an angry response.

Maybe it was an emotional reaction to extreme thirst, or maybe they felt betrayed by Moses and God when they didn't find the water they expected to be there. Perhaps they were just frustrated or fearful. Regardless of the origin of the complaint, their conclusion was unmistakable: Moses, at God's direction, had brought them out of Egypt into this desert spot to kill them with thirst, and they had had enough.

They were done with Moses, his God, and his pie-in-the-sky talk about a Promised Land flowing with milk and honey. They couldn't care less about milk and honey. They needed water, and they wanted it now. This was no peaceful protest where they walked in circles holding picket signs and chanting slogans. This was an angry, violent lynch mob looking for someone to blame for their problems. If they couldn't quench their thirst with water, they would do it with blood. I'm sure Meribah was an apt name for Moses to give the place—after all, he was there and the one in the crosshairs—but even its most extreme meaning, "quarrel" still feels like an understatement.

The other name, Massah, meaning "testing," reflects God's opinion of what happened. At first glance, the challenge posed by the Israelites in Exodus 17:7 doesn't sound all that bad. In fact, while their attitudes and actions were clearly unforgivable, God's intense reaction seems a bit shocking. Was He not sympathetic to their situation at all? Granted, they could have handled it better than throwing a temper tantrum, but wasn't their frustration understandable? They genuinely lacked water, which might not be a significant inconvenience for eternal, supernatural beings, but is a critical life-threatening issue for humans. True, they were wrong, no doubt; but wasn't God making this testing thing a bigger issue than it really was?

Part of the problem is that the force of Exodus 17:7 is softened in translation. When we frame a question like that in English, it implies the expectation of a positive answer. Consequently, we read it as, "Is the LORD among us, or not? Sure He is!" However, the context clearly indicates that this is a cynical statement that presupposes a negative response, so the intended tone is, "The LORD isn't among us, is He? If He is, you sure couldn't prove it by me." The word "tested" also seems to lack significance until we read Psalm 95, where God elaborates further on His perspective:

> For He is our God,
> And we are the people of His pasture and the sheep of His hand.
> Today, if you would hear His voice,
> Do not harden your hearts, as at Meribah,
> As in the day of Massah in the wilderness,
> When your fathers tested Me,
> They tried Me, though they had seen My work.

> For forty years I loathed that generation,
> And said they are a people who err in their heart,
> And they do not know My ways.
> Therefore I swore in My anger,
> Truly they shall not enter into My rest. (Psalm 95:7-11)

Loathing and anger are very strong words, especially when spoken by God. To say He was unhappy with them would be a gross understatement. They had done more than merely try His patience—they had challenged His very presence among them. They dared to accuse Him of more than just not showing up; they claimed He didn't even exist. It didn't matter that they had just walked through the Red Sea on dry land along a path several miles wide, with walls of water hundreds of feet tall on either side. It made no difference that the entire Egyptian army, the most formidable fighting force in the world at that time, had drowned before their very eyes in a matter of minutes. They didn't care that they had been spared from the ten horrific plagues He had inflicted upon Egypt, including the slaughter of every firstborn.

The miraculous sweetening of the poisonous waters at Marah, just three days after crossing the Red Sea, meant nothing. The manna and quail that had literally fallen from the sky every day for at least the past six weeks—and that they had filled their angry bellies with on the very day they went hunting for Moses' head—didn't prove a thing. Jehovah wasn't real. Jehovah was a farce. Jehovah, and everything about Him, was a lie.

"They provoked *Me*," God says. "They tried *Me*. I didn't test them; they tested *Me*. Massah was only the beginning. For forty years, I provided for them every single day, and they still complained. For forty years, I fed and protected them. I even ensured their clothes and sandals never wore out. But it was never enough. No matter what I did or how consistently I did it, they still questioned My word, doubted My promises, and claimed that I didn't even exist. That's why I got angry. That's why I swore they would never enter into My rest."

That's crazy, isn't it? Can you blame God for being angry? What more could those ingrates want for proof? He wasn't just asking them to trust an ancient promise He made to their ancestors 500 years earlier. He didn't reference how faithful He had been to Abraham, Isaac, Jacob, or even Joseph, for that matter, even though they were carrying Joseph's bones with them as they traveled, which were a clear and obvious testimony to that fact. They didn't even have to think back to the prior year. They had seen all of it with their own eyes—the plagues, the Red Sea, the water, the manna, the quail, all of it—in the last six months, and much of it in the last sixty days. Yet, when they reached Rephidim, they were so angry and so fed up with the very idea of God that they wanted to kill Moses.

The emotional intensity in this story is shocking and staggering. I'm dumbfounded by how the Israelites could be so upset with God, oblivious to the miracles happening right before their eyes every single day. How could they possibly deny God's existence and goodness when they had seen so much? I just don't understand it.

However, if I'm completely honest with you, myself, and God, I must admit that I do understand them because I've been them. My grumbling and quarreling with God have been just as intense and irrational as theirs was. I've never complained about not having water, but I have complained about other things I felt were equally essential to my life, yet just as insignificant in relation to His power and plan. I've been frustrated and despondent over His seeming lack of care for me and my life, despite volumes of evidence to the contrary, simply because I didn't like where I was or what I thought He was doing to me at the time. In many, if not most, of those occasions when I felt He was testing me, I was actually testing Him. I tremble just thinking about the sheer audacity I've had to take that same tone with the living God and shudder at the numerous times I've done it.

If that wasn't enough, the term used to describe my testing of God carries some vitriol as well. The words for "trial," "tried," and "testing" in Hebrews 3:8-9, as well as "tempted" in Hebrews 4:15, are the same words found in James 1, but the word for "provoked" does not appear anywhere else in the New Testament aside from Hebrews 3. It means "to embitter" or, depending on the voice, "to be or cause to be rebellious." While it's one thing for me to rebel against God, the idea that my choice not to wait well could lead Him to rebel against me was extremely sobering. Here's some free advice: if you're going to pick a fight with someone, choose someone your own size—someone much, much smaller than God.

Think about what happens in our model when we turn the testing towards God. Sure, He can withstand anything we might throw at Him, but that's hardly the issue. Instead of our character being validated, we assassinate His. Wasn't that what the Israelites did in Exodus 17:7? Instead of expressing faith, we openly declare our mistrust in Him. This, by necessity, destroys hope, because we are not just questioning His goodness; we are firmly asserting that He is not good. Without hope, our waiting becomes a ponderous chain that drags us into despondency and despair. This, in turn, only strengthens our negative attitude towards God, proving that the cycle operates just as effectively in reverse as it does in the direction it should follow.

I had never stopped to appreciate the intensity of God's anger towards the provocation of the Israelites on that day, and how incredibly terrifying and foolish a posture it was and is to take towards the

God of the universe. I was mortified when I contemplated the fact that the complaining I felt I was entitled to do, and the moping about my circumstances I thought was justified were actually reckless and severely ill-advised attempts to flip the tables on Him, pointing my scrawny little accusatory finger in His direction, just like they did.

No buts about it

With those sobering thoughts in mind, the answer to our question about what waiting well means is almost self-evident.

> For who provoked Him when they had heard? Indeed, did not all those who came out of Egypt led by Moses? And with whom was He angry for forty years? Was it not with those who sinned, whose bodies fell in the wilderness? And to whom did He swear that they would not enter His rest, but to those who were disobedient? So, we see that they were not able to enter because of unbelief. (Hebrews 3:16-19)

Do you want to know what rest is and what it means to wait well? Ok. Do you remember what happened at Massah and Meribah? Yeah, not that.

It's not just the grumbling, griping, and complaining. Don't get me wrong: those are bad, but they are merely symptoms of a much more serious underlying problem. The opposite of rest is what the author repeatedly characterizes throughout this passage as hardening one's heart. The verb "to harden" in Greek is *skleruno*, the same word from which we get terms like arteriosclerosis or hardening of the arteries. The imagery is very clear and appropriate. Hardening of the arteries occurs when plaque from fat and cholesterol builds up on the interior walls of the arteries, restricting and eventually completely blocking the flow of blood. Similarly, hardening of the heart happens when layers of plaque, in the form of unbelief and disobedience, build up on the walls of our hearts, restricting and eventually choking off hope. He even takes things a step further and calls a hardened heart as something we would never want to use to describe ourselves: evil (Hebrews 3:12).

That's very strong language, and it's extremely hard to swallow. God couldn't possibly be intimating that dreading my wife's next round of chemotherapy because the side effects might land her in the hospital again is unbelief, could He? Surely, He isn't implying that worrying about how I'm going to pay the mortgage and the even larger health insurance premium while I'm without any income is disobedience, is He? He isn't seriously suggesting that if I become offended and frustrated with people who constantly lie about me and treat me poorly, I'm the evil one, is He?

Of course not. He isn't intimating, implying, or suggesting anything. He's stating it outright.

> Be anxious for nothing, but in everything by prayer and supplication with thanksgiving let your requests be made known to God. And the peace of God, which surpasses all comprehension, will guard your hearts and your minds in Christ Jesus. (Philippians 4:6-7)

There's no cancer exclusion clause in Philippians 4:6. I am commanded not to worry. About anything. Period. If I do, I'm declaring that I do not believe the peace of God will guard my heart and mind in Christ Jesus. From a human perspective, it may be understandable, but from a biblical hope perspective—from God's perspective—it's not. That's me flipping the tables on God. That's me saying that He's good for every situation . . . except this one. That's unbelief.

> For this reason I say to you, do not be worried about your life, as to what you will eat or what you will drink; nor for your body, as to what you will put on. Is not life more than food, and the body more than clothing? . . . Do not worry then, saying, "What will we eat?" or "What will we drink?" or "What will we wear for clothing?" For the Gentiles eagerly seek all these things; for your heavenly Father knows that you need all these things. But seek first His kingdom and His righteousness, and all these things will be added to you. (Matthew 6:25, 31-33)

Once again, this is a command. It's not optional. My responsibility is to make the kingdom of God my priority; His is to care for my needs. This isn't reassurance with caveats buried in some fine print of a contract. It's a promise from the One who made the world and everything in it, including me. When I choose to worry about my material needs, I've replaced His priorities with mine. Even worse, I'm saying that I expect the One who cannot lie to betray His promise. That's not just insulting; that's me provoking God. That's disobedience.

> You have heard that it was said, "YOU SHALL LOVE YOUR NEIGHBOR and hate your enemy." But I say to you, love your enemies and pray for those who persecute you, so that you may be sons of your Father who is in heaven; for He causes His sun to rise on the evil and the good, and sends rain on the righteous and the unrighteous. For if you love those who love you, what reward do you have? Do not even the tax collectors do the same? If you greet only your brothers, what more are you doing than others? Do not even the Gentiles do the same? Therefore you are to be perfect, as your heavenly Father is perfect. (Matthew 5:43-48)

Tell me if you've heard this before: this isn't a suggestion. I am to love my enemies and pray for those who persecute me. If I don't, I'm just like them. Even worse, I'm saying that God doesn't know what He's talking about, and I do. That's me hardening my heart. That's evil.

Before you say or even think another "yeah, but," let me stop you right there and encourage you to take a look at the summary of the author's argument in Hebrews 3. It is so important to him that he states it twice. Listen to his heart and his reason for calling out both them and us about our unbelief.

> But Christ was faithful as a Son over His house—whose house we are, if we hold fast our confidence and the boast of our hope firm until the end. Therefore, just as the Holy Spirit says, "TODAY IF YOU HEAR HIS VOICE, DO NOT HARDEN YOUR HEARTS AS WHEN THEY PROVOKED ME." (Hebrews 3:6-8)

> For we have become partakers of Christ, if we hold fast the beginning of our assurance firm until the end, while it is said, "TODAY IF YOU HEAR HIS VOICE, DO NOT HARDEN YOUR HEARTS, AS WHEN THEY PROVOKED ME." (Hebrews 3:14-15)

Don't let that little word "if" trick you into thinking that these verses suggest the possibility of being able to lose your salvation, because the point being made is exactly the opposite. The Greek structure is awkward, especially when trying to be as literal as possible in translating it into English, which is what makes it difficult. The key to these verses is understanding that the word for "if," *eanper*, doesn't indicate doubt but rather emphasizes a strong expectation that the hypothetical statement is true. Therefore, Hebrews 3:6 should be read as follows: "If we really hold fast to our confidence and our hope (and I believe we do), then we are the house of God, which means we do not harden our hearts like the Israelites did at Meribah. The house of God does not act that way—that's out of character for us." The same holds true for Hebrews 3:14: "We have become partakers of Christ, and I know that includes you, too, even if you're feeling fearful. Do you know what partakers of Christ do? They hold on to their assurance until the end. Do you know what they don't do? They don't harden their hearts. They don't provoke God. They don't shrink back and curl up."

This was not some legalistic warning that if they didn't perfectly respond in faith and hope to every test, they would be out of the club and on a one-way ticket to the lake of fire, regardless of everything else. That's basically the falsehood the Judaizers were teaching. Instead, this was intended to be a pep rally for folks who were in a dire situation and a spiritual funk, who were wondering if God had forgotten them, and possibly if He even existed. "No!" he cries. "Don't think like that. That's hardening your heart like those fools at Meribah did. That's not you. That's not what you were taught, that's not what you believed, and that's not who you are. So don't act like it is."

When you're in a challenging period of waiting, taking a hard line like this can seem harsh. Waiting is hard, frustrating, and frequently painful. We are humans, not robots, and feelings are part of who we are. Are we supposed to act as if the challenges we face don't affect us? Are we not permitted to acknowledge disappointment, weariness, or loss? Are we unbelieving, disobedient, and evil if we have a bad day?

Of course not. God created us not only with the ability to experience these emotions, but with the express intention that we would. I believe that, as beings created in God's image, we feel emotions because God does. We know that God experiences frustration and anger: Massah and Meribah are a prime example of this. We also know that God is holy and does not sin, so clearly feeling negative emotions doesn't necessarily equate to sinning. How then do we reconcile our tendency to lament and dread waiting with the commands to not be anxious and to wait with eagerness and joy without being rebellious towards God?

In the middle of the conversation about rest in Hebrews 3 and 4, there are a couple of verses that seem wildly out of place. Ironically, they are likely the most familiar and frequently quoted verses in these chapters, yet I doubt you've ever heard them quoted in the context of waiting or rest.

> Therefore, let us be diligent to enter that rest, so that no one will fall, through following the same example of disobedience. For the word of God is living and active and sharper than any two-edged sword, and piercing as far as the division of soul and spirit, of both joints and marrow, and able to judge the thoughts and intentions of the heart. And there is no creature hidden from His sight, but all things are open and laid bare to the eyes of Him with whom we have to do. (Hebrews 4:11-13)

What do entering into rest and not following the example of disobedience have to do with the penetrating characteristics of the word of God? Plenty.

Every parent recognizes that their child has different cries. A cry of pain differs from one of fear. A cry when they're sick sounds distinct from when they're tired or angry. The differences may be indistinguishable to those who aren't the child's parent or who haven't tuned their ear to hear them, but they do exist. What makes them unique is the thought and intent behind the cry.

From infancy, we possess the ability to express what is in our hearts and minds, even before we understand and can articulate words. Ironically, as we become more skilled in communication, we often try to conceal and mask our true thoughts and feelings. Some of this is a valuable practice, stemming from respect and consideration for others' ideas and emotions; however, much of it serves as a coping or defense mechanism that helps us navigate or evade uncomfortable situations. Consequently, it is common for us to end up confusing or misleading ourselves, leaving us unsure of what we truly think or feel.

It's appropriate for me to be concerned about my wife's health and feel troubled by the idea of her spending five days in the hospital due to a bad reaction to chemotherapy. At what point does that concern shift from an expression of a loving husband's heart to one of unbelief that provokes God? When does being worried about paying the bills change from a sign of responsible stewardship to a reflection of a disobedient heart? How can I discern if the anger and frustration I feel towards those who abuse me and others is righteous indignation or evil vengeance?

The answer to questions like these is that exposing your heart to the Word of God reveals on which side of the line you stand. Its razor-sharp edges can split the finest of hairs, and God will use it to expose the true intentions and thoughts of your heart—not to embarrass you or put you in your place in front of others, but for your own awareness. Verse 13 says that nothing and nobody escapes His gaze. Everything is open and laid bare to Him, literally, "naked and held by the throat." According to verse 11, the context for this revelation is rest. The result is that you avoid following the example of disobedience set by the Israelites at Massah and Meribah, because through His Word, God will either validate the thoughts and intentions of your heart as pure or correct them.

Rest, therefore, functions like a thermostat for how well you're waiting. It doesn't just register the temperature of your heart, it regulates it, keeping you from the extremes of shrinking back from God or trying to wrestle control from Him. It creates time and space to call your attention to your attitude and perspective, helping you understand if you're waiting well or if you need to make an adjustment. If you can't put the weight of your waiting down, even for a moment, because of worry, fear, or a desire to control, that's a sign of unbelief and disobedience that will accumulate over time like plaque in your heart, hardening it. Likewise, if you are carrying it well, it not only confirms that but also provides you with a safe place to set it down for a while.

Rest is also how we clear the plaque of unbelief and disobedience from our hearts.

> For indeed we have had good news preached to us, just as they also; but the word they heard did not profit them, because it was not united by faith in those who heard. For we who have believed enter that rest. (Hebrews 4:2-3)

The word "united" means "to mix together." When you mix the word of God with faith, you enter rest, which is the opposite of hardening one's heart. There's nothing magical or mystical about this. Every time you combine the word of God with faith, you find rest. Every act of faith is an act of belief, making it an act of obedience, which is good. That's the complete opposite of unbelief, disobedience, and evil. Each time you rest, you benefit from it. Unbelief is repelled by belief, disobedience by obedience, and the hardening of the heart by rest. This isn't about building a balance sheet to try to outweigh the bad with the good. Salvation doesn't work that way, nor does sanctification. This is about building character, fundamentally changing who you are and how you live your life. When you're at rest, you obey not because you're commanded to, but because that's who you are.

The repetitive nature of rest

Rest also has an interesting temporal nature. There is a past element of rest. God rested because He had completed His work (Hebrews 4:3-4). He has set down His barber's scissors. Additionally, there is a future element, too. "There remains a Sabbath rest for the people of God" (Hebrews 4:8-9). That's a significant part of our hope, isn't it? We've already discussed how we are not yet complete, but a day is promised when we will be.

However, there is also a present element of rest, and this is the aspect that the author emphasizes persistently, almost ad nauseam. Today, today, today. Rest isn't just a reminder of the past or a hope for the future; it is a reality to be entered into today. You can't just rest once and expect that it will carry you indefinitely. "Encourage one another day after day, as long as it is still called 'Today,'" he says. It's designed to be repeated, day after day after day.

The element of repetition was built into the concept of sabbath rest from the very beginning, as it is inherent in the concept of a week. While other significant units of time (days, months, years) have an astrological basis (Genesis 1:14), weeks do not. Instead, the defining event for a week is rest. It's not surprising that Jews, Christians, and Muslims recognize that God established the week at creation. What is interesting, however, is that although most of the world credits the Babylonians with establishing the seven-day week, the fundamental concept behind the cycle remains rest.

In the 1930s, the Soviet Union under Joseph Stalin, implemented what was known as *nepreryvka*, or the "continuous working week."

This idea was first proposed by Yuri Larin, a Soviet economist, with the goal of transforming the Soviet workforce into a powerful production machine that would elevate the Soviet Union to be on par with the other industrial powers in the world. The original idea was to institute a five-day workweek where each worker would work for four days and then have a day off. By staggering this schedule among the population, 80% of the workforce could be active every day. However, the experiment did not yield the intended results, as both people and machinery broke down more often and were not nearly as productive as Larin had theorized. Within two years, Soviet leadership reverted to a five-day workweek with a common rest day for everyone on the sixth day. By 1940, they had completely abandoned *nepreryvka*, returning to the traditional weekly structure of six days of work followed by a common day of rest.

More significant than the fact that the seven-day week proved to be the most productive cycle is that even when the Soviets implemented shorter weeks, they still distinguished them by rest days. In fact, particularly in the early days of *nepreryvka*, the odd, syncopated schedule was so confusing that colorful calendars were printed and distributed to the workforce so they could keep track of when they were supposed to work. The instructions printed on one of these calendars in 1930 read, "Memorize your color, and you will always know your day of rest." Even the productivity-obsessed Soviet Union, one of the most anti-God governments in modern history, instructed their workers to measure their weeks, not by their labor, but by their rest.

However, the emphasis on time in Hebrews 3 and 4 regarding sabbath rest focuses not on the week, but rather on the day—specifically, this day, today. That's odd because we've just established that the sabbath ended a seven-day cycle. Is there any precedent in Scripture for days other than the seventh being considered sabbaths? As a matter of fact, there is.

In Leviticus 23, we read about the institution of the annual feasts that the Israelites were to observe. Even adhering to a strict calendar of lunar months, each consisting of 28 days, the sabbath math gets thrown off almost immediately. Moses starts by reiterating that every seventh day is to be a sabbath. The Passover was to be celebrated on the 14th day of the first month—so far, so good. However, the 15th day began the seven-day Feast of Unleavened Bread, with both the first and seventh days also designated as sabbaths. The 16th day represents the Feast of First Fruits, which is not a sabbath, but it does begin the countdown of 50 days to the Feast of Weeks, a sabbath that, due to the way the Israelites were to count time, inevitably never falls on the seventh day.

Additionally, the Day of Atonement was fixed on the 10th day of the seventh month, and the seven-day Feast of Booths started on the 15th day, with the first and eighth days observed as sabbaths. Then, in Leviticus 25, we learn that the land itself was supposed to have a sabbath rest for an entire year every seven years. Every 50 years featured an additional, special sabbatical year known as the Year of Jubilee. The point is that, even under the Mosaic law, sabbaths were not limited to once every seven days.

Resting daily

Is it really possible to rest every single day? According to the author of Hebrews, it is not only possible; it is essential.

> But encourage one another day after day, as long as it is still called "Today," so that none of you will be hardened by the deceitfulness of sin. (Hebrews 3:13)

The deceitfulness of sin is never off the clock, and it doesn't recognize vacations or holidays. You don't get to choose when your faith will be tested, nor how long your seasons of waiting last. Every time we mix Scripture with faith, we enter into rest, and since we need to do this daily to face the challenges of each day, we must rest every single day. The beauty of this is that if you fail to rest today, you can still rest tomorrow, when it becomes today. That's not meant to provide an excuse for a lack of rest; rather, it's meant to ensure that rest is always available to you.

The importance of the daily aspects of waiting and hope, of resting and faith, cannot be overstated. The weight of waiting does not come from instantaneous traumatic events; rather, it comes from the accumulation of relatively minor things that grow into heavy weights over time. Acting out of self-dependence and unbelief for even one day can quickly compound these loads.

No one was more familiar with this reality than the prophet Jeremiah. He bore the dubious honor of informing the nation of Judah that they would be taken into captivity for 70 years due to their extensive disobedience to the Lord, evidenced by a backlog of 70 sabbatical years they had failed to honor (Jeremiah 25:11, 2 Chronicles 36:20-21). The book of Lamentations expresses Jeremiah's sorrow and anguish over this punishment and the state of affairs in Judah that made it necessary. In chapter 3, he relates how this punishment has affected him personally. Read the first 18 verses and see if they don't perfectly mirror how you have felt on those days when your whole world was falling apart. He even leans into the idea of God rebelling against him when he says in verse 3, "Surely against me He [the Lord] has turned His hand repeatedly all the day."

In the middle of all this despair are some of the most encouraging and life-giving verses in the entire Bible. Pay attention to Jeremiah's shift from the weight of his lament and what triggers it.

> He has filled me with bitterness,
> He has made me drunk with wormwood.
> He has broken my teeth with gravel;
> He has made me cower in the dust.
> My soul has been rejected from peace;
> I have forgotten happiness.
> So I say, "My strength has perished,
> And so has my hope from the LORD."
> Remember my affliction and my wandering, the wormwood and bitterness.
> Surely my soul remembers
> And is bowed down within me.
> This I recall to my mind,
> Therefore I have hope.
> The LORD'S lovingkindnesses indeed never cease,
> For His compassions never fail.
> They are new every morning;
> Great is Your faithfulness.
> "The LORD is my portion," says my soul,
> "Therefore I have hope in Him."
> The LORD is good to those who wait for Him,
> To the person who seeks Him.
> It is good that he waits silently
> For the salvation of the LORD. (Lamentations 3:15-26)

Notice that when Jeremiah's strength perished, so did his hope (Lamentations 3:18). What brought it back? Remembering that God is faithful and that His mercies and compassion are new every morning.

And where was he, and what was he doing while he remembered those things? He was waiting silently (verse 26)—he was resting. How did he know that God's mercies and compassion were new every morning? He wouldn't have, unless he was seeking them and paying attention to see that they were there every day. He had to. There is no way that any man could feel what Jeremiah expressed throughout the book of Lamentations and retain hope if he isn't stopping every day to unload his pain from his chest and lay it at the feet of God Almighty, resting in the promises of God's faithfulness, mercy, love, and grace. Jeremiah did not live to see the day that God's people returned to the land and rebuilt the temple and the wall around Jerusalem, but he lived each day with hope because he rested daily in the faithfulness of God.

The enhanced Waiting Wheel

By now, you may have noticed a recurring theme. The weight of my waiting is not dependent upon the significance, severity, or intensity of the circumstance in which I find myself. The progression of my dependence on God's character resulting in me becoming more like Christ gives purpose and meaning to waiting, but I only experience the full effect if I have the right perspective. My attitudes about the waiting process directly affect the benefits I receive from it.

If my hope is anchored in the goodness of God, I wait eagerly; if it's not, I set myself up for disappointment and disillusionment. Joy infuses a sense of welcome anticipation into the actions I take based on that hope, because I know that my faith will hold up under testing. Although the trials themselves are not pleasant, understanding them as discipline intended to produce perseverance and maturity, rather than punishment and pain, enables me to face their repetition with rest, as I experience God's proven character being reproduced in me.

This, in turn, leads to greater confidence in His character and an even surer hope in the next cycle.

These four attitudes—eagerness, joy, discipline, and rest—are like the spokes of a wheel connecting our waiting to hope, faith, perseverance, and character. They are the key to alleviating the weight associated with waiting. Without them, you may still be able to experience some growth, but you will not be able to shed the crushing heaviness waiting can bring. When you start to feel frustrated and trapped in a quagmire of waiting, honestly evaluating your attitude against these four things will not only help you understand why you're struggling, but it will also guide you on how to correct it.

Only you and God can sort out why your waiting feels so heavy. What I can tell you is that when my waiting is characterized by fear rather than eagerness, it's because I'm doubting God's goodness in some way. When I don't look at my trials with joy, it's because I'm trying to hide a sin, and I know the test will reveal that I haven't been acting in faith. When I feel beaten down to the point of thinking I can't go on, my lack of endurance stems from becoming so focused on the immediate moment that I've forgotten what He has done for me in the past. When that happens, I need to discipline my heart and mind to view the situation from God's loving long-term perspective. When I become weary in my waiting, I've learned that it means I'm working too hard at working, trying to manipulate circumstances ultimately beyond my control, and not hard enough at resting, leaning into the arms of the One whose purposes cannot be thwarted.

The good news is that waiting well is a skill, which means you can learn to do it better. Even better news is that, because you are a finite being bound by time, you will have ample opportunity to hone and improve that skill continually. The one thing you never have to wait for is the opportunity to wait better. So, instead of getting discouraged when our waiting isn't characterized by eagerness, joy, discipline, and rest, let's talk about some things we can do to change that.

Chapter Seven
How to Wait Better

Hope is meaningless unless it is real. If it doesn't make a difference, if it doesn't work—every time, everywhere, in every situation, without fail—it's not worth holding onto. Yet, it's one thing to understand and appreciate the beauty, power, and peace that changing your perspective on waiting can bring to your life: it's something completely different to experience those changes in reality. As difficult as waiting can be, changing how you wait can be even harder. Moving away from anxiety and worry to hope and rest takes more than just inspiring words and interesting word studies. It demands a change in your mindset, priorities, and approach to life. It takes discipline. It takes practice.

So where do you start? How do you break out of thought patterns and behaviors that make you want to step back and curl up, and instead embrace new ones grounded in hope and faith that can withstand challenges? There are no magical incantations that will change this for you overnight, but there are several practical things that I have found very helpful on this journey in my own life.

Become convinced of the goodness of God

> And without faith it is impossible to please Him, for he who comes to God must believe that He is and that He is a rewarder of those who seek Him. (Hebrews 11:6)

This is where it all started for me, and I find it hard to imagine how anyone can develop true biblical hope without it. I don't know where you stand on the issue of God's goodness, but unless and until you become convinced that God is good because that's all He can be, none of the rest of what we've looked at matters. Without that truth as the cornerstone of your thinking, your hope will eventually fail—not because God ever fails, but because you will revert to trying to control things yourself. When you rely on your own ability to control your circumstances, that's not hope; hope is confidence in things unseen, and you are very visible. No matter how successful you may feel or how confident you are in your own abilities, we all have our limits, and your world will break down when you reach yours.

How can you become convinced of the goodness of God? Hebrews 11:6 puts it succinctly: you must choose to believe that God exists and that He is good. If you don't, there is no argument that can change your mind and no evidence that can be presented to persuade you. However, if you've made it this far in this book, chances are you are at least willing to consider the idea that God exists and that He is good. In fact, perhaps you genuinely want to believe this but find it difficult to do so. Identifying with Hebrews 11:6 doesn't guarantee that your struggles with waiting evaporate immediately, but it does provide the necessary foundation on which to build.

As overly simplistic as this sounds, start by consistently affirming the goodness of God. Say it out loud. Write it on your bathroom mirror with a dry erase marker. Do whatever you need to do to keep that truth constantly in front of your eyes and at the top of your mind. Behaviorists say that it takes, on average, 66 days to develop a new habit, so commit to being intentional about asserting that God is good for two months. Memorizing and reciting Psalm 119:68 is a good way to do this: "You are good and do good; teach me Your statutes." Ten simple words—that's it. Phone numbers are 10 digits; if you can memorize your phone number, you can memorize the 10 words in that verse. Personally, I needed to extend the thought a bit further, so the phrase I adopted was, "God is good because that is all He can be, and God does good because that's all He can do."

Regardless of how you verbalize it, it is important that when you feel the weight of a moment, a situation, a test, or a challenge, you consciously choose to say, "I don't know how this will turn out, but regardless of the outcome, I believe God is still good. I reject any perspective or interpretation that would suggest otherwise. I may not know what it means, but I do know what it doesn't mean. It doesn't mean that God has stopped being good."

As you allow that fundamental premise to take hold in your heart and mind, you will find yourself viewing situations differently than before. Whether you're standing in line at a government office or facing a life-and-death situation, you will not only see the many good things the Lord brings into your life every day, despite the challenges you face, but you will also begin to view affliction itself as good (Psalm 119:71). This shift occurs because you will have learned to look forward to the positive transformation that affliction brings.

Take resting seriously

> Therefore, let us fear if, while a promise remains of entering His rest, any one of you may seem to have come short of it. For indeed we have had good news preached to us, just as they also; but the word they heard did not profit them, because it was not united by faith in those who heard. (Hebrews 4:1-2)

Waiting is a function of time, making it inescapable. It is something that just happens. You rarely have any control over waiting. Resting, on the other hand, does not just happen. You must choose it. The author of Hebrews isn't telling us to be afraid of anything but is telling us not to underestimate the importance of resting. When he warns us about falling short, he's talking about shrinking back and curling up, our instinctive response to uncomfortable situations. Doing that is dangerous because it causes us to harden our hearts. Hardened hearts lead to situations like Massah and Meribah where we rebel so vehemently against God that He rebels against us. Not only is that extremely serious business, but it's also a fight we can't win.

As a result, we have to prioritize the idea of resting. Observing a day of rest once a week has its practical benefits, but its most important benefit occurs when we stop and put down the burdens we've carried throughout the other six days. What you choose to do or not do on your day of rest is far less important than the posture of your heart when you're resting. Just because you attend church on Sundays doesn't mean you're truly resting. It may indicate that you're choosing to stop working and worrying about life's challenges, but that's not a guarantee. Like the proverbial strong-willed child who was told to sit in time-out yet complied with reluctance, you might still be defiantly exclaiming, "I may be sitting on the outside, but I'm standing on the inside!"

In their book, *Worship: Rediscovering the Missing Jewel,* authors Ronald Allen and Gordon Borror state that "the real factor in worship is a heart desire for God; the reason it fails to occur in the pew is because it fails to occur in the routine of daily living."[31] I am convinced the same is true for rest. While the focal point of the creation story is on the seventh day (and appropriately so) when the entire day is dedicated to rest, we must not overlook that every other day of the week also contains a rest period. The phrase "the evening and the morning" that delineates the other six days not only incorporates evening, the natural period of rest, in each of them, but places it first. To this day, Jews begin their days at sundown, not sunrise, meaning that the first thing they do every day is rest. I'm not suggesting we need to change how we count and measure time, but I am suggesting that, as the author of Hebrews exhorts us, we must give rest a prominent place in our hearts and minds, and that will in turn alter the way we live our lives.

Practicing rest daily is essential for maintaining a hopeful perspective. It includes setting aside time to sit quietly and reflect on the goodness and faithfulness of God, as Jeremiah did, but it is not limited to that. Hebrews 4:2 tells us that the proper way to fear God, and thereby give rest the necessary priority, is to mix the word of God together with faith in our hearts. I believe Scripture memorization is essential to being able to do this effectively. Many people shy away from memorizing Bible verses because they feel they aren't smart enough or are intimidated by some of the unfamiliar sentence structures in certain Bible translations. I would submit that memorization has nothing to do with intelligence or education—it's merely a function of discipline and repetition.

About twenty years ago, I was summoned for jury duty. In that particular county, jury duty lasted an entire week. Jurors were expected to show up every day and wait until they were called to sit in a pool of prospective jurors for a trial. Those who were not chosen were not released but had to return to the waiting room and became candidates for the next pool. As it turned out, I was never seated on a jury, so I spent the entire week in the waiting room. This was before Wi-Fi was generally available, so our entertainment options were limited. One other person and I chose to work on a puzzle set up on a table beneath a TV mounted on the wall. During the afternoons, as my companion and I worked on the puzzle, a group of about a half-dozen other people watched the soap operas playing above our heads.

I quickly discerned the die-hard fans from the casual viewers in the group because they knew everything about the shows. It was almost comical to listen to them passionately bring the less-informed viewers up to speed on all the ins and outs of the ridiculous storylines—not just of one show, but all of them. They couldn't have been more invested and passionate about these unrealistically contrived plots if they actually lived in those fictional towns, and sometimes it was hard to tell whether they believed they did.

The sheer volume of useless and irrelevant information these people had about a world that didn't exist was astounding. How did they become masters of such trivia? They engrossed themselves in it every day. Some of the ladies who were more casual viewers knitted or crocheted while they watched, but not the die-hards. Their soaps were way too important for them to be distracted by anything else.

If you stop to analyze your patterns and habits, you may find that your inability to memorize effectively is more from a lack of prioritization and consistency than from mental acuity. If you want to tackle long passages, an entire chapter, or even a whole book, knock yourself out. My grandfather was able to do that. I had the opportunity to travel to Jerusalem with him, where we visited the Dome of the

Scroll, which displayed the scroll of the book of Isaiah discovered in the Qumran caves. To illustrate that ancient Hebrew is nearly identical to modern Hebrew, our guide had a member of our group point to a random spot on the scroll, and then he began translating it into English. Almost immediately, my grandfather recognized the passage and cited the chapter and verse. While he was exceptionally intelligent, it wasn't just his mental abilities that allowed him to identify the passage our guide was reading. It was the countless hours he dedicated to reading and studying Isaiah because it was one of his favorite books of the Bible.

However, the point is not to attempt to master large chunks of memorized material. The objective is to flood your heart and mind with the word of God so that it permeates your thinking, as the book of Isaiah did for my grandfather and as the plots did for those soap-watching jurors.

One effective way to increase my exposure to the Scriptures is a technique taught to me years ago by a dear friend and mentor, Rich Ferrell. I noticed that he used very long computer passwords but never seemed to have difficulty remembering them. When I asked him for his secret, he explained that he used a Bible verse or a portion of one as a mnemonic device. He had a system (which he did not share with me) for representing words in the verse with letters, numbers, and special characters, making it as simple as reciting the verse in his head to remember the password. Not only was it easy for him to remember and extremely difficult for others to guess, but this method also had the added benefit of forcing him to actively focus on that verse each time he entered a password.

In these days when we have passwords for everything that require greater length and complexity, and that must be changed more frequently, I can't think of a better way to consistently expose your mind to God's word. I'm sure the system I use is different from the one Rich used, but I have certainly reaped all the benefits from the practice he followed. I can't tell you how centering it has been during periods when everyone and everything seemed to be against me to have to think, "He who dwells in the shelter of the Most High will abide in the shadow of the Almighty" (Psalm 91:1) a dozen times or more each day as I logged into a computer.

Whether I was coming out of a meeting with a colleague who had a difficult attitude, facing a technical problem I didn't have an answer for, or falling behind on a project with a looming deadline, the two or three seconds it took to run that Scripture through my mind to my fingers gave me a moment of rest to pause, set down the burden of the moment, remember who is actually in charge of my life, and then return to the task at hand with a more hopeful perspective. While nothing can replace dedicated quiet times for studying the Scriptures, meditating on them, and praying, even if you struggle to find time for those things, you can still enter into rest just by changing how you log into a computer.

Hurry up and wait

> Therefore let us be diligent to enter that rest, so that no one will fall, through following the same example of disobedience. For the word of God is living and active and sharper than any two-edged sword, and piercing as far as the division of soul and spirit, of both joints and marrow, and able to judge the thoughts and intentions of the heart. And there is no creature hidden from His sight, but all things are open and laid bare to the eyes of Him with whom we have to do. (Hebrews 4:11-13)

The Greek term for "be diligent" means "to make haste, urge on, hurry," so the phrase "be diligent to enter rest" would have sounded to a Greek speaker like "hurry up and wait" does to us in English. I personally think the play on words in Hebrews 4:11 is intentional. Often, when we use that expression, it indicates frustration driven by the fact that no matter how much effort we put forth, we can't make something happen faster or reach a resolution more quickly. It's a sarcastic way of expressing exasperation, while hoping the comic play on words will mask how irritated we really are.

Of course, the author of Hebrews has something completely different in mind. In passages like 2 Timothy 4:9 and 21, and Titus 3:12, when Paul urges his coworkers to be diligent, he's telling them to hurry, or as the NASB translates it, "make every effort" to come see him. He expresses the same sentiment when he tells the Thessalonians that he was "all the more eager [diligent] with great desire to see your face" (1 Thessalonians 2:17). Although *apekdechomai* isn't used, the tone in Paul's words reveals a hint of it. I think that same sentiment of making every effort with eager anticipation is also expressed in Ephesians 4:3, where Paul urges the church there to be "diligent to preserve the unity of the Spirit in the bond of peace." Therefore, when we combine the ideas of diligence and rest, the expression reads, "make every effort to stop working," implying that we should maintain an attitude of joyful and eager anticipation while we do so.

Hurry up and wait. Make every effort to stop working. Those exhortations would sound even more contradictory and nonsensical if they weren't so true. Instinctively, the last thing we want to do is wait. Unfortunately, by trying to avoid waiting, we are essentially saying that we'd rather wait to wait than do the original waiting in the first place. If that sounds confusing, it's because it is, and it's as pointless as it is ridiculous. However, when I take a 20-minute detour to bypass a 10-minute traffic jam because I prefer the illusion that going faster means I'm making more progress, that's exactly what I'm doing.

Similarly, forcing ourselves to stop so we can rest isn't easy. The demands on our time and attention to keep working—whether that's responding to employment-related obligations or our own self-imposed to-do lists—build momentum. We discover that Newton's First Law of Motion applies to emotional and metaphysical weights as much as it does to physical ones. Both waiting and work possess mass, and once they gain momentum, they tend to steamroll our minds and lives. Stopping them, especially when they've acquired substantial weight, is difficult. It takes focused and intentional effort.

However, sometimes, taking the detour is the better option. Sometimes, the situation calls for determined persistence to keep working, and resting is merely an attempt to justify laziness and procrastination. Sometimes, it can be hard to tell the difference between eagerness and anxiety and between working and resting, even in one's own heart.

In the physical world, according to Sir Isaac Newton, the determining factor in whether a force contributes to momentum or inertia, to work or rest, is the direction in which the force is applied. In physics, this idea is represented by vectors, which indicate not only the magnitude of the force but also its direction and angle relative to other forces at play. In the spiritual world, the intentions of the heart are comparable to vectors. While the amount of energy is important, the intent behind it—where it is directed—determines whether the effort moves me toward rest or away from it.

When producing a procedural crime drama, a screenwriter can leave clues that reveal a perpetrator's intent when committing the crime, but life in the real world isn't scripted that way. Jeremiah 17:9 states, "The heart is more deceitful than all else and is desperately sick; who can understand it?" It's so challenging to identify intent that half of the time we don't even understand why we do the things we do. This is why Hebrews 4:12-13, which on the surface seem wildly out of place in this context, are in fact pointedly appropriate. The Word of God can distinguish between what you merely thought about doing and what your intent was. Can you discern where your soul ends and your spirit begins, and vice versa? God can. As the creator and architect of the universe, He not only has all the blueprints, but He drew them up Himself.

While the fact that no one is hidden from His sight and that everything is an open book to Him serves as a warning against the futility of pretending to rest while secretly trying to control our world, I think the author intended this to be an encouragement. When we feel the weight of our circumstances, we frequently say and do things that are harsh, towards both others and God. At what point do those actions become sin, and when do they not? Frequently, the truth is that no one can truly tell, not even ourselves. No one, that is, except God; and He says His word can help us make that distinction.

This is yet another benefit of consciously and purposefully mixing the word of God with faith in your heart. The Scriptures are sharp enough to split even the finest hairs, exposing whether your intentions are right or wrong, and whether your work is directed at working or resting. Although your cry of anguish may be indistinguishable from your cry of anger to anyone but God, He still knows whether you are coming to Him with open palms of desperation seeking mercy or with clenched fists of rebellious control looking to provoke Him—even if you're not sure yourself.

However, even with your thoughts and intentions sorted correctly, how do you actually go about the process of stopping? We saw in Hebrews 3:18-19 that the Israelites at Massah and Meribah did not enter rest because of unbelief and disobedience, which the author also mentions in Hebrews 4:11. You enter into rest—you shut it down and settle in—by believing and obeying. "Believe what? Obey what, specifically?" you may ask. The answer is simple: you believe and obey whatever the soul-penetrating word of God tells you to. Any of it. All of it. At any given time, the rough edge that our Father, the master craftsman, is working on in my life will be different from the one He's concentrating on in yours. The process for all of us, however, is exactly the same. In the words of the familiar hymn penned in 1887, by John H. Sammis, it works like this:

> *Trust and obey, for there's no other way*
> *To be happy in Jesus, but to trust and obey.*[32]

Seize hope

Three times in Hebrews 3 and 4 we are exhorted to "hold fast." This word does not convey the idea of tying a knot at the end of your rope to try to hang on just a little while longer because you are slipping. Instead, it conveys the idea of a strong and violent, seizing action. It means to hang on with both hands fiercely determined not to let go. What we are told to hold onto that way, in all three passages, is hope. Notice also that each exhortation is grounded in our relationship to Christ. In Hebrews 3:6, we are His house; in 3:14, we are partakers of Him; in 4:14, He is our great high priest. The world tells us to seize the day; the Bible tells us to seize our hope in Christ.

What does seizing hope look like in the real world? We can find practical applications in each of these three passages.

Make joy the governing principle of your life

> But Christ was faithful as a Son over His house—whose house we are, if we hold fast our confidence and the boast of our hope firm until the end. (Hebrews 3:6)

Did you catch how the phrase "the boast of our hope" in Hebrews 3:6 aligns with "we exult in hope" in Romans 5:2? Joy can be a passive emotional response to experiences, but in Scripture, it is primarily an act of the will, a choice. Coming to grips with the reality that you are not obligated to respond to bad or unpleasant circumstances in your life with anger, fear, and frustration can be hard, especially when those feelings have been ingrained over a long stretch of time, particularly in toxic and unhealthy relationships. Without minimizing the complexities of healing from these experiences, at their core lies this simple truth: because of the regenerative power of Jesus Christ, you have a choice. You can respond with joy instead of anger, fear, and frustration by simply choosing to do so.

If you are struggling to choose joy over fear during your waiting, I strongly encourage you to spend time immersing yourself in Romans 8. It offers much insight on changing your mindset and highlights many benefits we have because we are in Christ, such as being "heirs of God and fellow heirs with Christ" (Romans 8:16). It discusses how to pray when you don't know what to ask for and reveals how Paul worked through the challenges he faced while learning to wait eagerly. Spend enough time there, and you will find a hook on which you can hang whatever reservation you have that keeps you from choosing joy.

As I've said before, the crux of my issues with waiting was the goodness of God. Even now, there are days when I'm challenged to doubt that truth. When that happens, I turn to Romans 8:32 to help me turn sorrow into joy.

> He who did not spare His own Son, but delivered Him over for us all, how will He not also with Him freely give us all things? (Romans 8:32)

If God was not only willing but actually sacrificed His Son for me when I was His enemy, what possible reason could He have to withhold any other good thing from me? If that doesn't make it easier to choose joy, I'm not sure what else will.

Encourage others to wait eagerly

> But encourage one another day after day, as long as it is still called "Today," so that none of you will be hardened by the deceitfulness of sin. For we have become partakers of Christ, if we hold fast the beginning of our assurance firm until the end (Hebrews 3:13-14)

Mike Tomlin, head coach of the Pittsburgh Steelers, is a master motivator. He is well-known even outside the football world for his pithy and sometimes quirky statements that effectively communicate his philosophy in meaningful and memorable ways. One of these is, "We want volunteers, not hostages." This means he prefers players who genuinely want to be on his team and are willing to buy into his system and the team's culture, rather than those who are merely going through the motions. He values a less talented player who is eager to contribute as part of the team more than a highly talented player who isn't committed to the organization's values.

Volunteers and hostages are apt analogies for the two ways we can view ourselves in seasons of waiting. The folks mentioned in Hebrews 11 were volunteers, while the Israelites at Massah and Meribah definitely thought of themselves as hostages. Volunteers eagerly wait because they understand it is good; hostages rebel against it and attempt to escape by controlling it because they believe it is bad.

How do you convert hostages into volunteers? According to Hebrews 3:13, you send them to recruit more volunteers. "Encourage one another day after day, as long as it is still called 'Today,' so that none of you will be hardened by the deceitfulness of sin."

Keep in mind that the people being addressed here were shrinking back. They were being held hostage by pain, confusion, and fear. They doubted God's goodness. The whole reason the book of Hebrews was written was that they were losing their hope, their faith, and their nerve. They were waiting horribly. Yet, instead of expecting them to master waiting on their own, the author admonishes these hostages to look one another in the eye and encourage the other guy to become a volunteer.

One of the greatest dangers of waiting is isolation. There's a reason why imprisonment is a punishment in our society, and solitary confinement is the most extreme form it can take. We are designed for community, and when we are removed from it, we become crippled. When I encourage someone else, it not only helps pull the other person out of their isolation, but it also pulls me out of mine. If I encourage you to make joy the defining principle of your life, I'm implicitly committing myself to the same standard and exposing myself to you holding me accountable for it. As Jesus famously pointed out, we often find it much easier to address the splinter in someone else's eye than the log in our own. When our goal is to find fault with others to make ourselves look and feel better, that's a bad thing; but when it's motivated by encouragement and love, it becomes equally powerful in building up both parties.

Don't let the fact that your actions don't match your words intimidate you. I'm not saying your inconsistency doesn't matter, because it absolutely does. It matters a lot. What I am saying is that you shouldn't allow your inconsistency to justify isolating yourself. Embrace community and seek accountability as you wait by first encouraging someone else who is struggling just as much or even more than you are. In fellowship, both of you will learn to wait more eagerly.

Romans 8 can be helpful in this regard as well. As Hebrews 3:14 points out, we are partakers with Christ. He wasn't a hostage; He volunteered to enter fully into the thick of our pain, struggle, and waiting. Study Romans 8 and make a list of all the different ways Paul identifies that we are partakers with Jesus and tell me you're not encouraged by it and that it doesn't make you wait more eagerly. Then, find a friend and share what you just discovered with them. It will change both of your lives.

Make it your goal to persevere, not just survive

> Therefore, since we have a great high priest who has passed through the heavens, Jesus the Son of God, let us hold fast our confession. For we do not have a high priest who cannot sympathize with our weaknesses, but One who has been tempted in all things as we are, yet without sin. (Hebrews 4:14-15)

The notion of being a survivor is quite common in the world of chronic diseases like cancer, or when referring to those who have experienced various forms of trauma yet have not succumbed to it. Being a survivor in these contexts is heralded as a positive thing and is often worn as a badge of honor. In certain instances, it represents a vital step towards liberation from harmful individuals and situations. If you or a loved one proudly wears that badge, I do not intend to belittle or devalue the importance of your trauma or your recovery.

Nonetheless, as admirable and honorable as survival may be, as illustrated in Romans, James, and Hebrews, the objective is not merely to survive but to persevere, which I believe the Scriptures affirm is a loftier and more satisfying goal.

Survivor language often measures success by what hasn't been lost rather than what has been gained. Phrases like "I just want it to be over," "Hurry up and get it over with," "It could have been worse," and "I don't care anymore—I'm just done" focus on minimizing negative impact. We even deceive ourselves to make surviving sound more noble with statements like, "What doesn't kill you makes you stronger," when, in reality, we know that most of the time, what doesn't kill you simply leaves you with just enough strength to wish it had.

Sometimes we try to spiritually "pretty up" those kinds of remarks by quoting passages like Romans 8:37: "But in all these things we overwhelmingly conquer through Him who loved us." However, in many cases, we end up minimizing the last five words of that verse or dropping them altogether. This not only reduces a statement about perseverance to survivor language but also turns it into the worst kind of survivor language: egocentric and controlling.

The issue with survivor thinking and speech is that it contradicts the expected outcomes of testing. We understand this from the reason given in Hebrews 4:15 for why we should hold fast to our confession. Jesus was tempted in all things just as we are, yet without sin. It's important to remember what sin in this passage is associated with: unbelief, disobedience, and hardening of the heart. These are all binary things: either you believe, obey, and find rest, or you don't. There is no sliding scale, no grading on a curve. There is no room for merely surviving—you can't be defeated in every phase of the game but then catch a lucky break in the final minute or your last at bat and win. When Jesus was tested, He didn't just do enough to barely get by and survive; He aced the tests. He didn't just win; He conquered. That victory is reaffirmed every time our faith is tested and proven, every time we persevere.

This third and final instance of the "hold fast" exhortations in Hebrews 3 and 4, while still encouraging us to maintain a determined, firm grip on our confession, carries a less violent and more gentle connotation in Greek than the first two. It acknowledges that waiting, along with everything it entails, is hard. It recognizes our deep desire to live in hope, with our lives characterized by the eager anticipation of promises made by a God we know is good and loving, but it also acknowledges that consistently doing so is not easy.

It admits that when push comes to shove, there can be a lot of shoving, and that it frequently takes everything we have just to stand. Over the course of multiple encounters like this, survival becomes seemingly the only realistic objective, because as soon as we weather one storm, another is immediately upon us—and that's only if we're lucky enough to face them one at a time. However, Jesus shuts down that way of thinking as false because He was tempted "in all things as we are," which means He not only faced every kind of test, but He also dealt with every mode of delivery for those tests, including being piled on, but He didn't sin. He didn't just survive; He conquered.

The word "tempted" in Hebrews 4:15 is the same as the various "trials" mentioned by James. As you may remember, although the intent of the trials we face may be constructive or destructive, when those tests are applied to faith rooted in biblical hope, the only result is perseverance. This means becoming more like Christ. It means not just surviving; it means conquering, just like He did.

Remarkably, when the author of Hebrews brings his whole argument to a climax in chapter 12, he points his readers and us toward the example of Jesus Himself, emphasizing these same three "hold fast" principles.

> Therefore, since we have so great a cloud of witnesses surrounding us, let us also lay aside every encumbrance and the sin which so easily entangles us, and let us run with endurance the race that is set before us, fixing our eyes on Jesus, the author and perfecter of faith, who for the joy set before Him endured the cross, despising the shame, and has sat down at the right hand of the throne of God. For consider Him who has endured such hostility by sinners against Himself, so that you will not grow weary and lose heart. (Hebrews 12:1-3)

Notice that Jesus' attitude was not driven by obligation or fear, but by joy. The phenomenon of the Father turning His back on the Son at the cross, because our sin was placed on Him, must have produced a level of pain that is inconceivable to us, even in our most vivid imagination. The way Jesus endured that was not by focusing on the pain of the moment but on the joy of what lay ahead. Just as Jacob viewed his seven years of labor as if they were nothing because of his love for Rachel, Jesus despised the shame of the cross, only much more. That's what making joy the governing principle of your life looks like. You become so concentrated on hope and becoming like Christ that the weight of all the waiting and testing seems inconsequential.

In the immediate context of Hebrews 12, the "cloud of witnesses" refers to the list of people in chapter 11. However, when you consider the broader message of the whole letter, it seems to include the exhortation in Hebrews 3 for the recipients to encourage one another. In a community, both with those who have gone before you and those who are around you today, you gain perspective and benefit from their examples. Even if you're skeptical that no one else can identify with your plight or truly know how you feel, remember that Jesus was tested in every way we are—only to a greater degree and with better outcomes. He created faith (and thus also waiting and hope) and perfected living by faith.

Throughout my wife's cancer journey, we have been struck by the prevalence of cancer. It affects nearly everyone you encounter, yet it's remarkable how isolated and alone cancer patients and their families often feel. Interacting with others facing similar challenges has revealed that some are in better and others in worse conditions than we are, and that we can both provide support and receive help from one another. Using your struggles to uplift others lightens the burden, not just for them, but for you as well.

Perfecting faith. Enduring the cross. Despising shame. Sitting down at the right hand of the throne of God. That's not survivor language—it's conquering language. A survivor mentality comes from focusing too much on the opposition and not enough on hope, and the author intentionally draws our focus to how Jesus absolutely dominated sin to ensure we would not grow weary and lose heart. Regardless of how bloody our fight might get, we will never strive to the point of shedding our blood for the sins of the world. Paul says, "If God is for us, who can be against us?" (Romans 8:31) Just remember that He doesn't make us strong so we can conquer in our own strength, but so we can overcome "through Him who loved us" (Romans 8:37).

Pray with confidence

My grandfather was very particular about his tools. He didn't mind letting others use them as long as they were used appropriately, returned in good condition, and put back exactly where and how they had been found. I still remember the severe tongue lashing I received for leaving a hammer on the workbench instead of returning it to its place on the pegboard above. It was a mistake I only made once.

During my freshman year in college, I spent an autumn Saturday afternoon watching football on TV at my grandparents' home while they were away on a trip when my uncle John came in and said he needed my help. He had been using my grandfather's lawn tractor and trailer to haul limbs and leaves from the yard and dump them into a partially dried sewage lagoon at the bottom of a steep embankment. Of all my grandfather's tools, the lawn tractor was his pride and joy. Unfortunately, when Uncle John was backing this particular load of debris to the edge of the hill above the lagoon, he had gotten it too close. The ground gave way underneath the wheels of the trailer, sending the lawn tractor, with him on it, tumbling backwards down the 150-foot slope, ultimately landing on its side in eight inches of muck.

Uncle John had managed to jump clear of the tractor and only suffered a few bruises and minor abrasions. The tractor, however, did not fare nearly as well. The hood was severely dented in several places. The steering wheel, being the highest protrusion, had taken the brunt of the force when the tractor flipped over and was contorted in several different directions. One of the front wheels was noticeably pigeon-toed with respect to the other. The hitch to the trailer was so twisted I had no idea how he had separated it from the tractor, but somehow, he had before he came to get me.

The first thought that ran through my mind as I surveyed the wreckage was, "Dude—you are so dead. Your father-in-law is going to kill you." After the dressing down I had received for slightly misplacing a hammer, I was horrified at the thought of what would happen when Grandpa saw the condition of his beloved lawn tractor. As I helped him flip it up on its wheels and push it out of the mud, I began to wonder how much trouble I would be in for just helping him, even though I had done nothing to contribute to the accident.

When we got the tractor back to the house, Uncle John used the garden hose to wash off the mud while asking me to fetch a hammer. I thought better of reminding him to return the hammer when he was done. It wasn't going to matter anyway—he was already as good as dead. I returned to watching the football game because I didn't want to be anywhere near the scene of the crime, but I could still hear him pounding away uselessly at the dents in the hood. When he finally came back inside, I asked him what he was planning to do. He shrugged and said, "I'm going to call him and tell him what happened."

I wasn't sure whether that decision was more courageous or foolish. However, Uncle John apparently knew better than I did because when he got off the phone, he told me that Grandpa hadn't chewed him out at all. Instead, Grandpa's immediate concern had been for his son-in-law's safety, not for his tractor. When Grandpa returned from his trip a couple of days later and saw the condition of the tractor, they had the same conversation again. I was astounded by the confidence Uncle John had to come clean about what he had done and the mercy he received in return. Uncle John paid for the parts, and he and Grandpa ended up working together to repair the tractor. What I thought would be a serious blow to their relationship turned out to bring them closer together.

Even the most positive and optimistic among us struggle with projecting the same image onto God that I projected onto my grandfather. More days than we care to admit, we doubt the goodness of God, work harder at working than at rest, and try to pull ourselves up by our own bootstraps instead of seizing hope. In moments when

I gather enough courage to honestly examine why the weight I'm carrying is so heavy, I find a surprisingly large amount of it comes from guilt. I knew what I was supposed to do or not do, and I did the opposite. My faith was tested, and I blew it. I didn't persevere. Not only do I know this, but I also know God knows it, too. I also know that I should talk to Him about it, but I really would rather not have that conversation right now—you know what I mean?

However, as I learned from my Uncle John, the time we need to approach the Father is precisely after we've rolled the lawn tractor down the hill into a cesspool and mangled it beyond recognition. Instead of trying to hide our failure or pretending we have everything under control and staying away from God, we need to approach Him with confidence, bent steering wheel in hand, seeking help. He promises us mercy (that we will not receive the condemnation we deserve) and grace (that we will receive blessings we don't deserve), especially in the hour we need them most.

Therefore, learn to have honest and direct conversations with God. Approach Him with confidence, knowing that nothing you say or do can jeopardize your standing before Him. He already sacrificed His only Son on your behalf while you were still His enemy (Romans 5:8-11), so what more could you possibly do to turn Him away from you?

If you have confidence to approach but don't know what to ask for, He will also help you with that.

> In the same way the Spirit also helps our weakness; for we do not know how to pray as we should, but the Spirit Himself intercedes for us with groanings too deep for words; and He who searches the hearts knows what the mind of the Spirit is, because He intercedes for the saints according to the will of God. (Romans 8:26-27)

Consequently, there is really no excuse. The only reason for not praying is that you choose not to. Pray with confidence, not because the act itself holds any magical properties, but because of the power of the One who answers your prayers according to His will because He loves you.

Epilogue
The Wait Continues

From 1976 until his death in 2009, radio broadcast personality Paul Harvey regaled audiences worldwide six days a week with stories about famous people or events, highlighting little-known or forgotten facts. He was a master storyteller, capable of engaging the imagination without revealing the identity of the person or event until the very end. After delivering the punchline, he would conclude the story with his signature catchphrase, including an iconic pregnant pause: "And now you know . . . the rest of the story." I loved the way Paul told his stories, and I enjoyed the challenge of figuring out who or what he was describing before he revealed it.

As I sit here today, I wish I could do my best Paul Harvey impersonation and tell you . . . the rest of the story, but I can't. Not only do I not know anything about your story, but I also can't bring closure to my own. Crystal still has cancer, but I have no more insight into when that journey will end than I did several years ago when she received the metastatic diagnosis. There are good days when it's hard to tell that she's sick at all, and then there are days when I'm constantly reminded of its unavoidable reality. I'm still waiting for several other long-term challenges to resolve. I also understand that when they eventually come to an end, new ones will take their place.

In the meantime, I've witnessed other seasons of waiting begin and I've seen some end. Some have occurred in my own life, while others have unfolded in the lives of those around me. Many of these stories have had happy endings; several have made me sad, and others have left me with mixed emotions. For the most part, they have been good, because I've learned to discern the hand of the Lord at work more clearly. However, there are still plenty that leave me puzzled, unable to grasp what God has in mind. The bad ones are more apparent since it is often clear when I and others are not trusting in God's goodness, but instead are shrinking back and curling up. Yes, without a doubt, those are the hardest to watch, because I now see them as reenactments of the rebellion at Massah and Meribah. However, unlike historical battle reenactments where the carnage is fake, these conflicts are very real, as is the spiritual, emotional, and sometimes physical damage that accompanies them. Thankfully, God and His promises never change, and there remains time to wait in hope, act in faith, build perseverance, choose joy, and find rest.

I've thought a lot about how I would answer Greg now if he were to corner me behind a bowl of chips and dip at a party and ask me again how I'm dealing with the weight. The heaviest part of the weight is still the wait, but I'm waiting much better today than I did back then, so I don't feel the same way I once did. I'm better at recognizing tests of my faith for what they are, and I've developed more perseverance, so I get frustrated and flustered less often. My determination to make joy my governing principle has increased, and every now and then, I actually catch myself being eager. In fact, there's a particular situation in my life right now that I've been struggling with for many months, which looks like it may soon be over. I've encountered

The Wait Continues

several major setbacks in that journey, and it's been difficult for me to wait eagerly. Yet now, as that season appears to be coming to an end, I'm feeling a bit nostalgic. As odd as it sounds, I think I'm actually going to miss that test when it's gone—specifically, I'm going to miss the waiting. Perhaps that's another way to experience *apekdechomai*—I don't know.

I have not yet arrived. Far from it. I still struggle with waiting and sometimes doubt the goodness of God. When I do, I have to go back to Psalm 119:68 and go through all the steps again. I have to remind myself that hope requires waiting and that waiting is good because it is essential for both faith and rest. I have to reassess what I can control and what I cannot, and I have to choose to be comfortable with both categories again, even though I've made that choice before. That said, the contentment and rest I have experienced encourage me to keep working on improving how I wait, because I now know how much better my heart is when I wait well.

I encourage you to use this book as a foundation for building your own study and practice in developing the skill of waiting well in your life. As I worked through the passages and concepts I've written about in this book, I kept discovering new facets, different angles, and additional connections to other biblical truths—so much so that at times I wondered if I would ever be able to finish it. Quite frankly, it isn't finished, as there is still so much to explore and much more for me to learn. However, now when I find myself frustrated with waiting and wishing I didn't have to do it, I have a solid framework grounded in the Scriptures that quiets my soul, recalibrates my thinking, and relieves me of the weight of the wait. My prayer is that it will do the same for you.

Endnotes

1. Alexander Pope, An Essay on Man, epistle 1, line 95, in The Poems of Alexander Pope, ed. John Butt (London: Methuen, 1963), 277.

2. Fyodor Dostoevsky, The Possessed (also known as Demons), trans. Constance Garnett (New York: Macmillan, 1916), part 2, chap. 1.

3. Friedrich Nietzsche, Human, All Too Human: A Book for Free Spirits, trans. R.J. Hollingdale (Cambridge: Cambridge University Press, 1996), 71.

4. Margaret Weis and Tracy Hickman, Dragons of Spring Dawning (Lake Geneva, WI: TSR, 1985), chap. 13.

5. George Savile, The Complete Works of George Savile, First Marquess of Halifax, ed. Walter Raleigh (Oxford: Clarendon Press, 1912), 33.

6. Francis Bacon, Apophthegmes New and Old, in The Works of Francis Bacon, vol. 14, ed. James Spedding, Robert Leslie Ellis, and Douglas Denon Heath (London: Longman and Co., 1870), 285.

7. Merriam-Webster, s.v. "hope," accessed December 4, 2024, https://www.merriam-webster.com/dictionary/hope.

8. Cambridge Dictionary, s.v. "hope," accessed December 4, 2024, https://dictionary.cambridge.org/us/dictionary/english/hope.

9. Collins Dictionary, s.v. "hope," accessed December 4, 2024, https://www.collinsdictionary.com/us/dictionary/english/hope.

10. Oxford Learner's Dictionaries, s.v. "hope," accessed December 4, 2024, https://www.oxfordlearnersdictionaries.com/us/definition/american_english/hope_2.

11 Leigh Harline and Ned Washington, "When You Wish Upon a Star," Pinocchio, directed by Ben Sharpsteen (Burbank, CA: Walt Disney Productions, 1940).

12 George Harrison, "Here Comes the Sun," Abbey Road, recorded by The Beatles, Apple Records, 1969.

13 Irene Cara, Giorgio Moroder, and Keith Forsey, "Flashdance... What a Feeling," Flashdance, directed by Adrian Lyne (Paramount Pictures, 1983).

14 Cara, Irene (May 20, 2013). «Electric Dreams: The Giorgio Moroder Story, Episode 2». BBC Radio 2 (Interview). BBC.

15 Whitney Houston, "Never Give Up," I Wish You Love: More from The Bodyguard, Legacy Recordings, 2023.

16 APA Dictionary of Psychology, s.v. "hope," accessed December 4, 2024, https://dictionary.apa.org/hope.

17 Colla, Rachel, Paige Williams, Lindsay G. Oades, and Jesus Camacho-Morles. ""A New Hope" for Positive Psychology: A Dynamic Systems Reconceptualization of Hope Theory."? Frontiers in Psychology 13 (2022): 809053. https://doi.org/10.3389/fpsyg.2022.809053.

18 Ibid.

19 Lopez, Shane J., and C. R. Snyder. The Oxford Handbook of Positive Psychology. Oxford University Press, 2009. https://doi.org/10.1093/oxfordhb/9780195187243.001.0001.

20 Lucy Maud Montgomery, Anne of Avonlea (New York: Grosset & Dunlap, 1917), 361.

21 Aristotle, Diogenes Laertius, Lives of Eminent Philosophers, trans. R.D. Hicks (Cambridge, MA: Harvard University Press, 1925), 5.18.

22 William Ernest Henley, Invictus, in This Singing World (New York: Louis Untermeyer, 1923), 333.

23 Roethlisberger, Ben and Te'o, Spencer. "Big Ben talks Footbahlin hiatus, 2024 Steelers preseason and more EP. 48." YouTube video,

58:17. Channel Seven, September 2, 2024. https://www.youtube.com/watch?v=NIaz4FnLLWU&list=PL78CoxFZXGKJIGjpR40ft2c0KnLdvnfmm&index=58

24 Maister, David H. "The Psychology of Waiting Lines." 2005. Accessed July 19, 2024. https://davidmaister.com/articles/the-psychology-of-waiting-lines/.,

25 Pollok, Scot. "The Father Sleeps." Reach Church, July 7, 2024, https://reachchurch.cc/sermons?sapurl=Lys4MjY5L2xiL21pLyt2dzg2a2h4P2JyYW5kaW5nPXRydWUmZW1iZWQ9dHJ1ZSZyZWNlbnRSb3V0ZT1hcHAud2ViLWFwcC5zaWJyYXJ5Lmxpc3QQmcmVjZW50Um91dGVTbHVnPSUyQjQ1YmZlMzE=.

26 Arndt, William F., F. Wilbur Gingrich, and Walter Bauer. A Greek-English Lexicon of the New Testament and Other Early Christian Literature: A Translation and Adaptation of Walter Bauer's Griechisch-Deutsches Wörterbuch Zu Den Schriften Des Neuen Testaments Und Der Übrigen Urchristlichen Literatur, Fourth Revised and Augmented Edition, 1952. Sixteenth impression. [Grand Rapids, Mich.]: Zondervan, 1974.

27 Alciphron, A. R. Benner, and F. H. Fobes. Digital Loeb Classical Library. Cambridge, MA: Harvard University Press, 1949. https://doi.org/10.4159/DLCL.alciphron-letters_book_ii_letters_farmers.1949.

28 Yale Center for Faith & Culture. "What Is Joy?." December 9, 2014, https://www.youtube.com/watch?v=4YjiJwUwMgA&list=PLO-6cjKGDlet70bQZVjSyl5dsRWfCCSAn&index=15.

29 Johnson, Russell. "Sunday Worship Service—10:30am." YouTube Video, 1:27:22. Faith Bible Church. October 13, 2024, https://www.youtube.com/watch?v=LdgyH_8RVts.

30 Ibid.

31 Allen, Ronald Barclay, and Borror, Gordon. Worship: Rediscovering the Missing Jewel. (Portland, OR: Multnomah Press, 1982), 24.

32 Hymnary.org. "Trust and Obey." Last modified November 4, 2024, https://hymnary.org/text/when_we_walk_with_the_lord.

www.ingramcontent.com/pod-product-compliance
Lightning Source LLC
Chambersburg PA
CBHW070547170426
43201CB00012B/1755